JEAN SIBELIUS

by **KARL EKMAN**

TRANSLATED FROM THE FINNISH
BY EDWARD BIRSE

JEAN SIBELIUS

His Life and Personality

✳

WITH A FOREWORD BY
ERNEST NEWMAN

GREENWOOD PRESS, PUBLISHERS
WESTPORT, CONNECTICUT

The Library of Congress has catalogued this publication as follows:

Library of Congress Cataloging in Publication Data

Ekman, Karl, 1895-
    Jean Sibelius, his life and peronality.

    Bibliography: p.
    1. Sibelius, Jean, 1865-1957.
ML410.S54E43 1972   780'.92'4 [B]   75-152594
ISBN 0-8371-6027-8

First American Edition, 1938 by Alfred A. Knopf, Inc.,
New York

Originally published in Finland under the title JEAN SIBELIUS,
EN KONSTNÄRS LIV OCH PERSONLIGHET

Reprinted with the permission
of Hulger Schildts

First Greenwood Reprinting 1972

Library of Congress Catalogue Card Number 75-152594

ISBN 0-8371-6027-8

Printed in the United States of America

FOREWORD

THERE have been biographies of Sibelius before this of Karl Ekman's, but his is the first to present us with something like the essentials of the portrait of the man. I say " something like the essentials " because we know, from previous experiences of the kind, that the first official or quasi-official biographies of great men are apt to be as remarkable for their reticences as for their revelations. We have to resign ourselves to that, for if it were not for these reticences there could be no first biographies at all. I am not, of course, suggesting that there is anything in Sibelius's life that needs to be hushed up: I doubt whether a world avid for " scandal about Queen Elizabeth " will ever have the thrill, blent of horror and delight, of learning that he ever robbed a bank, forged a cheque, or even committed a minor homicide. All I mean is that experience in these matters has shown us that in a first biography of any great artist a good deal that concerns his opinions of other people and his relations with other people has to be discreetly touched in with the

lightest of strokes, if only because there are intimacies
and susceptibilities on all sides to be considered. I am
not contending, then — nor, I fancy, would either the
author or the subject himself do so — that this book
of Karl Ekman's will be the final biography of Sibelius
fifty years hence. But I do contend that it is a work
of high value. All first biographies should be written
by someone with the entrée to the inner circle of the
subject — able, consequently, not only to extract illu-
minative reminiscences and avowals from the subject
himself but to tap, before it is too late, the memory of
those who were intimate with him in the formative
early and middle periods of his life. Ekman has had
special facilities for doing this; and so his book con-
tains a mass of hitherto inaccessible information that
is of the highest interest and value to students of
Sibelius.

The book is interesting not only because it furnishes
us with so many details, gathered at first hand, of what,
for all its relative seclusion from the greater world, has
been a life of immense energy, but also because it con-
firms at every point the impression of Sibelius the man
which those of us who have been studying him for the
last thirty years or so had formed from his music. We
now realize better than ever the strain of independence
in the man's personality that has made his music what
it is. External influences upon him have always been of

the slightest: he has passed through other composers' music, through contacts with contemporary artists, through public musical life in various European cities, calmly extracting from them all, with the unconscious sureness of an animal or a tree, just what he needed for nourishment and development in accordance with the inner law of his own being, and calmly rejecting the unassimilable remainder. His instincts have always been sound even when his procedure may not have been strictly logical. It was not strictly logical of him, for instance, to become an anti-Wagnerian at an early age on the strength of a rather limited acquaintance with Wagner's works — certainly long before he had seen any of them on the stage. But his instinct of repulsion from this music was sound enough: his was not the mind to find the right nourishment for its peculiar self in the Wagnerian drama, and it was in every way better for him to refuse from the first to make any attempt to incorporate so alien a substance into his own tissues. Few composers, indeed, show so few " influences " as Sibelius. He admits an unbounded admiration for Beethoven. But even Beethoven has not " influenced " him in the cruder sense of the word; he has merely provided him with an ideal of probity, simplicity, and logic in instrumental music, an ideal which Sibelius has pursued in a way of his own.

A good deal of the interest of this book resides in

the side-lights it throws on Sibelius's mental processes
as a composer. He has energetically denied that his
later instrumental works are program music; nor are
they, indeed, if we take that term in its more literal
nineteenth-century sense. But he has told us also that
the origins and the working-out of his musical thoughts
are determined by " mental images "; that is to say, his
work wells up from definite impressions of nature and
of human life, though he develops the resultant musical
ideas not in pursuance of any program that could be
put into words but according to their true nature *as
music*. We have only to read Ekman's book to see
how subtly interfused Sibelius's musical thinking has
been from the first with sight- and sound-stimuli and
with reactions to the impact of life upon him. Confronted, in later years, with what he wrote after hearing
Beethoven's F major quartet in the 1880's, he said that
but for the ocular evidence of his own letter to Wegelius he would have sworn that all this had been written
by someone else; he could no longer believe that while
listening to the quartet he had seen moonlight, a garden, a colonnade, birds of paradise, and so on, and
heard Beethoven sighing deeply, and God playing the
violin over large lakes of red water.

Many of us are apt, in our youth, to let our verbal
fantasy run away with us in this manner, though merci-

fully we shake off the disease so completely in later life
that we writhe in horror when we are confronted with
some purple patch or other written when we were under its influence. But the vital point, so far as Sibelius
is concerned, is not the actual verbal expression he gave
to the visual and auditory associations set up in him by
this particular quartet, but the fact that his mind was
fundamentally so constituted as to permit of the music
evoking associations of this order. For if a musician's
mind *is* so constituted it will work, by the very law of its
being, in both directions — not only will the music of
other men generate associations of this kind in him,
but associations of this kind will play a large part in
the generation of the music he himself writes. It is not
surprising, then, to find Sibelius dwelling as often as
he does, in the letters or the conversations recorded in
the present volume, on impressions derived from the
shapes or colors or sounds of things. Even after making some allowances for literary exuberance in Adolf
Paul's description of his friend's artistic processes as
a young man, it is clear enough that the musical faculty
of Sibelius has always been peculiarly susceptible to
external promptings. " For him," says Paul, " there
existed a strange, mysterious connection between sound
and color, between the most secret perceptions of eye
and ear. Everything he saw produced a corresponding

ix

impression on his ear — every impression of sound was transferred and fixed as color on the retina of his eye and thence to his memory."

The peculiar color of much of Sibelius's music — a color that seems low-toned to ears grown accustomed to the facile brilliance of most modern orchestral music — has been partly answerable for one persistent misunderstanding of him. In more than one quarter he is regarded as a " cold " composer. It is piquant, therefore, to learn from Ekman that his objection to the Danish writer Georg Brandes is that " he is too cold and clear, which is very much out of my line." The mistaken notion that Sibelius is cold — " bleak " used to be the favorite epithet of the critics — comes in part from the sobriety of the color of his music and the athletic spareness of its tissue, in part from the fact that he has always known how to keep a tight hand on passions that were really volcanic. In few composers has the Apollonian taken such controlling charge of the Dionysian as in Sibelius. Few, again, have evolved with so few deflections from the straight line of their destiny as he. He has had his period of *Sturm und Drang,* his romantic period, his period of pessimism, and finally a period of inner harmony in his last three symphonies, which he describes as " confessions of faith "; but throughout the quest has been of himself. It was greatly to his advantage that as a young man he grew up in what the larger musical world would regard as a provincial backwater. This provincialism made it easier for his genius, as a similar provincialism made it easier for the genius of Bach, to realize itself without distraction and without waste. Busoni was mistaken when he told his Vienna friends that the young man from Finland, " true to his northern origin, has developed later than we." He had really developed further already, in the sense that, thanks to his nature and to his relative isolation, he had accumulated fewer spiritual superfluities that would later have had to be scrapped. It is because Karl Ekman provides us with so much first-hand evidence of Sibelius's imperturbable progress towards his pre-appointed goal that this book is indispensable to anyone who would get to the secret of this great musical solitary.

ERNEST NEWMAN

PREFACE

𝕴 T IS NOT my intention in this book to enter into competition with the numerous responsible and subtle commentators who have analyzed and described Jean Sibelius the composer and his work excellently. I am attracted by a hitherto untrodden field and have devoted my interest to Jean Sibelius the man, the unique personality behind his work. Whenever I have found it necessary to discuss some of the creations of this master hand as especially typical of important stages of his life and of striking features of his personality, I have kept my analysis and characterization on the plane of common humanity.

An attempt to give a complete picture of Jean Sibelius the man calls for no excuse. Like every artist of a high order Sibelius has exerted an influence on his contemporaries far in excess of the limits of the direct effects of his art. As a proclaimer in music of the feelings and dreams of his people he has become a leading figure in the history of Finland, as a fearless combatant in the lists of universal musical art one of the great, whose struggle and purpose contributed towards forming the spiritual physiognomy of the twentieth century. What such a man experienced, how he viewed the personalities he met, how he wrestled with the problems that life set him, how he reacted to tendencies and events in various spheres of life — none of this can be a matter of indifference to his contemporaries.

Most of the materials of this book are the result of personal conversations with Sibelius in a dozen sittings lasting all day in his country home at Järvenpää, an hour's journey by train to the north of the capital of Finland. In our talks the master placed himself at my disposal with all the kindness of his generous nature without showing any sign of impatience at my persistent questions. I have endeavored as far as possible to express Sibelius's views of all that is important in his life — and even of what is less important when this has come quite naturally in the course of easy conversation — in his own words, either as I jotted them down on paper during our sittings or wrote them down immediately after, as the train steamed through the countryside of Nyland towards Helsingfors in the twilight.

During our talks in Järvenpää I had occasion more than once to recall that formerly Sibelius had consistently frustrated all attempts at inducing him to speak at all about himself and the reality that formed the background of his works; this attitude was due on the one hand to the *noli me tangere* of an aristocratic and susceptible nature towards the insistent outside world, and on the other to the spontaneous revulsion of a proud artist against the mere idea of being suspected of wishing to encourage public interest by any other means than his art. I must admit that I, too, failed to ascertain all that I and, no doubt, the reader would have liked to know. Guided by the lifelong conviction that the most profound and personal thoughts of an artist should be conveyed to humanity in his work, not in words and explanatory expositions, Sibelius preserved a reticence on many important points that it is my duty to respect. Sibelius maintained this reticence even about the most troubled periods of his life — when the financial troubles of a creative artist in such a small country as Finland threatened to assume overpowering proportions and when, in the struggle for his art, he had to suffer one crushing blow after another from uncomprehending critics. The picture of Sibelius's life will, therefore, appear brighter in some parts than it was in reality.

On such points as did not seem to me to be so important as to warrant trespassing on Sibelius's attention, but had, nevertheless, to be taken into consideration with a view to continuity and completeness, I have

obtained information from other sources. Finally, I
have, as far as possible, endeavored to bring color
and variety into this portrait of Sibelius by means of
the written and oral evidence of people who were in
contact with him at various stages of his life.

K. E.

Helsingfors
February 1935

CONTENTS

CONTENTS

CONTENTS

CONTENTS

ILLUSTRATIONS

NOTE

It was impossible to secure the originals of all the photographs of Jean Sibelius reproduced in this volume. As a result, it was necessary to reproduce the illustrations facing pages 52, 72, 102, 132, and 150 from halftones included in the original Finnish edition. It is hardly ever possible to make an adequate reproduction of a reproduction and these illustrations, therefore, are not up to the standard I try to maintain in Borzoi Books. Nevertheless, because of their intrinsic interest I have included these illustrations in this biography.

A. A. K.

JEAN SIBELIUS

I

PARENTAGE

Parentage — Descent — The death of his father —
His mother — His female relatives — Pehr Sibelius in
Åbo — Jean Sibelius the master mariner.

ON December 8, 1865 there was great joy in a
doctor's home in Tavastehus. A son had been
born into the world — the first boy in the family; two
years before, a daughter, the first child, had seen the
light of day. The happy parents were Dr. Christian
Gustaf Sibelius, senior physician to the Tavastehus
territorial battalion, and his wife, Maria Charlotta,
née Borg. The boy was christened Johan Julius Christian. To his friends and relations he was Janne (John-
nie), and Jean Sibelius was the name under which in
the fullness of time he was to go out into the world.

On his father's side the child was descended from
a family in the county of Nyland on the south coast
that had settled several generations earlier in the neighborhood of Lovisa, the town named after the Swedish

3

Queen Lovisa Ulrika. The family was of Finnish origin; the change from the Finnish interior to the Swedish coastal region had been made by a Finn belonging to the class of free peasants who had farmed their own land from time immemorial, who had moved with his wife from the parish of Artsjö to the coastal district of Lappträsk in the middle of the eighteenth century. In the course of time their descendants had adopted the Swedish language and customs, and the Swedish strain had recently been accentuated by Dr. Sibelius's father having married the daughter of a doctor who had immigrated from Sweden. On his mother's side Sibelius traced his descent from a family of soldiers, government officials, and clergymen, in which Finnish and Swedish blood had mingled in the course of centuries. The boy who saw the light of day in the town on the shore of Lake Vanajavesi was, therefore, undoubtedly of mixed extraction.

The question of Jean Sibelius's descent as a basis for theoretical speculations as to what nationality he should rightly belong to did not interest Sibelius himself in the least; in his opinion, environment, tradition, and personal conviction signify at any rate as much as descent, especially in a country where there is so much mixture of races as in Finland. As a character in which sincerity is the principal element, he has in his life and deeds unequivocally confessed his attitude towards the

battle of nationalities. Though coming from families
whose language and culture had been Swedish for generations, he associated himself enthusiastically in a
time of strong patriotic revival with the national Finnish movement and, with the unerring intuition of
genius, found means of expressing, besides the multiplicity of new musical values he gave the world's musical art, as genuine and convincing Finnish national
feelings and ideals in music as if they had come from
the depths of the Finnish people's soul. This whole-
hearted incorporation in the world of Finnish national
thought and feeling has been wedded unconstrainedly
to a noble personality's natural respect for the binding
sanctity of childhood's memories and family heritage.

This digression has led us away from the point we
started from. Let us return to the young man taking
his first faltering steps in the idyllic capital of Tavastland. It seems the right moment to let the subject of
our sketch speak for himself.

" I lost my father," says Jean Sibelius, " when I was
two and a half. Besides being physician to the battalion, my father had a private practice in the town of
Tavastehus and kept up the latter when the territorial
army was disbanded. He died in the exercise of his
duty. His life was ended by hunger typhus brought on
by the severe distress and failure of the crops in 1867
and 1868. He caught the infection while treating his

patients and died after a few days' illness on July 31, 1868.

" I have no recollection of my father's appearance or character. Strangely enough, the only thing that has remained in my memory is the purely physical sensation of his proximity during the times I sat on his knee and looked at my picture books. But as I grew up, I listened with avidity to everything that was said about him in order to form an idea of his personality.

" All that I heard about him testified to the liking and esteem that he enjoyed in Tavastehus society. As a doctor he was beloved by his patients, whose hearts he won by his friendly manner and his sympathetic character. He was also very popular in society; apparently scarcely any large dinner-party could be given without his being present. He played the guitar and had a good voice. During his schooldays in Borgå he had been one of the mainstays of quartet-singing in school, and as a student he was in the choir when *King Charles's Hunt*, the first opera written in Finland, was performed for the first time in Helsingfors in 1852.

" My father was a good man and a good friend. He had a large heart. I have had opportunities of reading letters that bear witness to his constant readiness to help his friends by word and deed. His was a cheerful and optimistic disposition, and in this respect he probably took after his father, Johan Sibelius, who was a

6

town councilor in Lovisa, and the first of the Sibelius family to settle in the town. My father presumably inherited his musical gifts from his mother, the daughter of a Swedish doctor, Mathias Åkerberg, who removed early in the 1780's from Skåne in Sweden to Lovisa, where he married; he ended his life as provincial doctor in Åbo.

" Having lost our father in our infancy, we children — my sister Linda, myself, and my brother Christian, who was three years younger — became all the more closely attached to my mother. Widowed at the age of twenty-seven, she bore her fate with brave resignation. She was fortified by her profound religiousness, which was far removed from all somber brooding over life; her views on life were bright and harmonious. She had a gentle and thoroughly feminine character. Very modest, she captivated all who got to know her well by her even, unruffled temper, her unaffectedness, her human sympathy. Wherever she went she was liked. My mother was the good angel of our home. She devoted herself entirely to the care of her children, she lived for us and with us. An unusually warmhearted being. It seemed as if it were her constant thought not to allow her loss to darken the childhood of her fatherless children.

" During our youth mother received excellent support from our maternal grandmother, Catharina Juli-

7

ana Borg, the widow of Gabriel Borg, the dean of
of Pyhäjoki. We spent the winters under the direct
supervision of our grandmother, for after the death of
our father we moved to her house in Tavastehus, where
she lived with her unmarried daughter Julia. Summer
meant a separation for shorter or longer periods:
Grandmamma spent the summer in Sääksmäki, in the
interior, where her sisters, Rosa and Inga Haartman,
owned the estate of Annila, while we went to Lovisa
on the coast.

"My grandmother was no common personality.
She went about constantly with a serious, not to say
severe look, but she had a decided sense of humor. It
did not take much to arouse it and then the severe
mask was cast aside in a moment. She was anxious that
we should not be spoilt, as we were, perhaps, inclined
to be by our mother, but Grandmother could never
be as strict with us as she wished.

"I still remember how, as a boy, I was caught by
her in some particularly glaring act of naughtiness — I
don't remember, however, what it was. I was prepared
for the worst. But she was content to look at me se-
verely and say, shortly and sharply: ' Janne! See that
this does not become a habit! '

"We had great respect for our grandmother, but
we knew, too, that we could count on her understanding when necessary. We got on extraordinarily well.

8

PARENTAGE

" Among the figures of my childhood I ought also to mention my paternal grandmother, Catharina Fredrika Sibelius, and my aunt Evelina, both of whom lived in Lovisa. They played a great part in my life, for until I was twenty-three we spent the summer with them either in Lovisa or among the islands outside it. They were uncommonly kindhearted beings, both very musical. I recall them with gratitude, chiefly for their motherly indulgence for my boyish pranks and escapades and their interest in my dawning musical talents."

Thus little Janne grew up in the loving care of female relations. But his childhood was not entirely devoid of male educational influence. He had an uncle, Pehr (Peter) Sibelius, for whom he had a great affection and whom he visited frequently, who was himself closely attached to the sons of his prematurely lost brother.

" My uncle Pehr was a business man in Åbo and was considered fairly well off for his time. He was very eccentric. His great passion was astronomy, after which came music. He constantly frequented the concerts of the Musical Society and played the violin assiduously. In his habits as in other things he was different from most people, for he put off his cult of music to the silent hours of the night. He usually began to play his violin at two o'clock in the morning.

9

" As a child and as a growing boy I often stayed with him in Åbo and enjoyed myself very much in his comfortable bachelor home. I found no great difficulty in adapting myself to his strange habits. Our relations were extraordinarily good.

" Music was the link that bound us, but he expected my future to lie in another direction. Astronomy was his dominating passion and he would have preferred both me and my younger brother to devote ourselves to that science. However, he raised no objections when I went in for music during my second year at college."

Sibelius's grandfather, the town councilor in Lovisa, had, besides the doctor and the business man, another son, the eldest, who had, indeed, died before Janne came into the world, but continued to live as a mysterious and fascinating figure in his nephew's childish imagination.

" My eldest uncle, Johan, went to sea in his youth and became a master and shipowner. He died of yellow fever in Havana two years before I was born. He was as little like the usual run of people as Uncle Pehr. He was very musical, and on his long voyages on the high seas he acquired a fund of reading of an extent and nature that was certainly unusual among sea captains of his time, and perhaps of all time. The letters of his that have been preserved testify to his refined interests and to a character of an uncommon kind. He

10

must, besides, have been a very temperamental gentleman, seeing that in a letter that is still in my possession my grandfather warns his son, the sea captain, against giving way to his violent temper.

"In Uncle Johan's youth it was still customary among the educated classes in Finland to use the French form for honorable Swedish Christian names. My uncle followed this custom and called himself Jean when abroad. When he started on his last long voyage, he left a parcel of visiting cards in his father's home with the name JEAN SIBELIUS. These visiting cards were taken care of and preserved with such devotion that a quarter of a century later I was able to use them when I made my entry as a young student into life in Helsingfors under the name of Jean Sibelius, originally intended as a kind of artistic name."

It is, therefore, from a Nyland sea captain, who was forgotten by later generations and died in the early 1860's in Havana, that the composer takes the name that he has made famous throughout the world.

II

A HAPPY CHILDHOOD

Tavastehus in the 1870's — The Russian element —
A country town devoted to music — Janne's first
steps in composition — Schooldays — Stories of a
friend of his childhood — A dreamer and lover of
nature.

TAVASTEHUS was a much livelier town in Jean Sibelius's childhood than it is at the present day. There was, indeed, not much left of the brilliant social life that had distinguished the small community during the childhood of the great painter Albert Edelfelt, who was eleven years older. Many of the leading families had moved away or retired, many an outstanding personality had died; among those who had left a blank was Jean Sibelius's own father, whose name is often mentioned in descriptions of social life in the Tavastland capital in the 1860's.

"I only saw the afterglow of this peculiar period in the history of Tavastehus," Sibelius relates. "But during my childhood and youth the life and people of Tavastehus still formed an environment that acted as a stimulus to an impressionable young mind.

" Above all, Tavastehus was a town of great culture. The life of the town was dominated by the landowners of the surrounding district, by officials and school staffs. There were no factories, commerce and trade did not predominate.

" A peculiar feature in Tavastehus was provided by the Russian army; when the territorial battalions were disbanded, a Russian garrison was established in the town. The Russian officers and their families brought a breath of another and larger world, which it was interesting to become acquainted with, and provided the good citizens of Tavastehus with much material for wonder and observation. The Russian element played an important part in the Tavastehus of my childhood, for at that time the relationship between Finns and Russians was not what it became later; both sides tried to maintain a good understanding. Tavastehus society did not close its doors to the Russian officers and their families. On the contrary, they were welcome guests at balls and evening parties, over which their bright uniforms, elegant manners, and Slav politeness shed a festive splendor.

" My friends and I made many good friends among the Russian boys. When I entered my teens, I was particularly intimate with a boy of fourteen called Kostya. I do not remember his surname, I only recall that his father was a colonel. Kostya had a very tender disposition, and we told each other our troubles and disappointments during hours of confidential talk. Kostya often visited our home and I, too, was at times a regular guest in the colonel's house. There I was once offered a delicacy I had not tasted before: bliny (Russian pancakes) as large as plates, and endless quantities of caviar. The first caviar in my life. I never spoke Russian with my friends. I did not even have to attempt to learn the language, for with the Russian's gift for foreign languages they soon picked up Swedish. There were also Russian families permanently established in Tavastehus, merchants and tradesmen who made a conscientious effort to accustom themselves to Finnish conditions. The attempt was most successful, especially as regards the younger generation. In the cosy atmosphere of the provincial town many small Russian boys became good Finnish patriots and recited Finnish patriotic poems with much feeling."

Tavastehus was not only a town of much culture, it was also a musical town. There was great love of music among educated families in the town, taste was well developed, and the Russian society in the town, inspired by every Russian's love of music, constituted a valuable addition to concert audiences. These found their satisfaction in the visits of the small orchestras from Helsingfors and Åbo, choirs from the capital, quartet societies, and the leading singers of the country.

The Sibelius children grew up in a musical atmosphere and themselves belonged to a musical family. I have already mentioned the musical gifts of their grandparents and aunt. On their mother's side, too, they enjoyed a rich musical inheritance. Their maternal grandfather, Dean Gabriel Borg, had been a good amateur violinist, and his love of music had been inherited by his daughters, Sibelius's mother and her sister, Julia Borg, both of whom played the piano well. The love of music in the growing generation was constantly kept alive by music being played in the home and was further encouraged by concert-going.

It was not surprising that Janne revealed musical gifts at an early age. When he was five he tried already to entice harmonies and series of tones from the piano's mysterious system of keys and strings. At the age of nine he began regular piano lessons. The piano did not attract him particularly — the violin was soon to arouse a great love in him. Instead of devoting himself passionately to learning scales and exercises, the boy lost himself in improvising on the piano and as a result he made his bow as a composer at the age of ten with a piece of descriptive music entitled Drops of Water, written for violin and violoncello pizzicato. At the same time he surprised his family by an excursion into the sphere of program music, a composition depicting " Aunt Evelina's life in music."

The members of the family watched these first groping attempts at composition with amused interest and gave their author every encouragement. But they were careful to avoid arousing any conceit in him that might have guided his course into perilous paths. It does not seem, either, that the budding composer claimed blind respect for his gifts. Music did not occupy a more than normal place in his childish consciousness.

Janne grew up a healthy child with all the interests, inclinations, and bad habits characteristic of it. His development had nothing in common with that of an infant prodigy. In view of what we know of him at a slightly older age we are entitled to assume that he was more sensitive, at times more introspective and dreamy, than children in general. But kind spirits had dropped healthy seeds in his soul that promoted the healthy growth and unperturbed harmonious development of his youthful mind.

The boy had a great love of nature and his relatives saw to it that it should be satisfied in rich measure. Up to his seventh year he was given a chance of breathing the healthy sea-air in the Lovisa neighborhood and enjoying the sight of the smiling shores of the Nyland skerries and the splendor of the wide, shimmering

bays. Afterwards the summer was spent either with relations near Lovisa or at Annila in Sääksmäki. Here
the more solemn Tavastland landscape of the interior
met the eye of the growing boy. But even during the years in which the summer was divided between Sääksmäki and Lovisa the greater part of the
season was spent at the seaside. And although, perhaps, the scenery of Tavastland left deeper traces in the
work of the grown man, the coast of Nyland proved an
incomparably greater attraction to the child.

" Lovisa was my sunshine and happiness, Tavastehus
was my school town, Lovisa was freedom. There I had
my grandmother and aunt, who simply worshipped me.
They approved of everything about me."

The greater intensity in the worship of his female
relatives probably played no small part in the boy's love
of their town. It was quite natural that his paternal
grandmother and aunt should obviously have spoilt
the boy more than his relatives on his mother's side.
They only had him for a few fleeting months in the
summer, whereas his maternal grandmother and aunt,
both of whom spent the winter in Tavastehus, saw him
for the greater part of the year.

When the summer of 1876 had passed, Janne experienced the seriousness of life for the first time. He had
been to a preparatory school and was now to start his
schooldays in earnest.

The choice of a school was of great importance for his future development. In the autumn of 1876 he entered the famous Finnish lycée that had its origin in the heated strife between Finns and Swedes in the 1870's.

Suomalainen Normaalilyseo, the "Finnish Model Lycée," later rechristened Hämeen Lyseo, the lycée of Tavastland, represented one of the first conquests of the victorious advance of Finnish culture — the fruit of self-sacrificing idealism and determined labor. The fact that at the foundation of the school political aims were wedded to zeal for education did not affect the level of this young educational establishment; it collected some of the best teachers the country possessed within its walls, and its far-seeing ideal set its own stamp on the whole of its work.

Suomalainen Normaalilyseo was a school of a special kind in other respects, too. The official imprimatur was Finnish, it is true, and so was its educational spirit, but many of the pupils came from Swedish homes. In a social sense, too, the classes were very mixed. Sons of the gentry from Tavastehus, Helsingfors, and other towns sat on the benches next to boys from the simplest of country homes; even Finnish children from Ingria were among the pupils.

Though the school and a great deal of the companionship the boy got through it were Finnish, his upbringing outside the school was still governed by impressions and educational impulses marked by Swedish culture. The family had literary interests to which the son responded. The books in the home contained treasures able to satisfy his growing love of reading. His soul was formed by poets who wrote in the Swedish language: Lenngren, Tegnér, Atterbom, Runeberg, Topelius, Rydberg. His absorption in their works during the time he was growing up laid the foundations of his appreciation of the delicate nature of poetry, of his sensitiveness to lyrical moods that was to bear such rich fruit in his future work.

The boy was very happy in this dual existence. There was no trace of conflict that might have arisen from the spirit of the school and the atmosphere in the home. His straightforward nature and active intellect enabled him to imbibe conflicting impressions and to combine them to the benefit of the harmonious development of his personality.

I have obtained a lifelike picture of Sibelius as a boy during the following years from conversations with Walter von Konow, who can claim to be one of Sibelius's oldest and most intimate friends. Being neighbors during the summer at the age of six in Sääksmäki, where Colonel von Konow owned the estate of Lahis, close to Annila, the boys were sent at eight years of age to the same preparatory school and passed on together from form to form in the Finnish school in Tavastehus. Walter von Konow was able to observe his friend's development at close quarters during childhood and youth. His narrative has the directness and value of first-hand knowledge.

"During his first years at school," von Konow relates, "Janne had a passion for acting. Almost every Saturday some of his schoolfellows were invited to act a play. The subjects were sometimes taken from the tales of Topelius and Andersen, but more often Janne's imagination provided the principal materials. Everything was left to the mood of the moment, inspiration, and chance. We never knew how the play was going to end. The action developed as the play proceeded, but there was always some ending under Janne's safe leadership. Janne played the parts of kings for preference in our childish plays.

"Then we started a children's orchestra, consisting of triangles, Jew's harps, clay cuckoos, and bells. Janne conducted from the piano. He was an extremely lively conductor, whose enthusiasm infected the whole orchestra.

"Janne was a lively and jolly boy, up to all kinds of jokes and pranks. But he would also suddenly fall a prey to profound melancholy. His temperament was uncommonly sensitive; his mood would change without any apparent external cause from the profoundest melancholy to the most care-free high spirits, when his jollity knew no bounds. He had very strong feelings.

" Janne was a great dreamer. He had a lively imagination that reacted easily to external impressions. It drew rich nourishment from his intense love of nature. He was fond of making long expeditions in the vicinity of Tavastehus and in the woods at Sääksmäki. His imagination endowed everything round him with life. In the dusk he amused himself by searching for fairy creatures in the darkest corners of the woods. If his imagination happened to be inclined towards gruesome things, it was at times quite uncanny wandering with him through a gloomy wood inhabited by hobgoblins and witches and other horrible things. It happened sometimes that our imaginations got so heated that, as darkness fell, we saw terrifying shapes appearing from their hiding-places Then we took to our heels as fast as we could. As we ran towards the safety of home, Janne would whisper in a gasping voice: ' I can hear steps behind us.'

" A beautiful sunset would evoke other moods of his imagination. We would sit for hours and gaze in silent wonder at the setting sun and the clouds shining in purple and gold — a whole fairylike world, full of magic and beauty, revealed itself.

" But Janne was not only the greatest dreamer in the school," von Konow continues, " he was also its greatest humorist. His extraordinarily developed comic sense was probably inherited from his grandmother. And when he described or witnessed an amusing episode, his laughter was so infectious that one could not help joining in.

" Janne was the undisputed leader of our childish games and frolics. His self-esteem was strongly developed, but it never showed itself in a way that might hurt his companions. He was far from being a bully; on the contrary, he was cordial, considerate, and sympathetic to an exceptional degree.

" Benevolence and kindness were among his most striking features even when he was small. If his heart was touched, he forgot all else in following its dictates. He was very generous. Once he was given some money by his mother for buying school-books. We started off together on this important business. On the way we met a poor old woman, who begged of us in miserable tones. Janne's heart melted; he gave the woman all his money, the book-buying had to be put off."

A dreamer, a being of imagination and feeling — that is the picture of Sibelius drawn by the friend of his childhood. But the mind of the dreamer was united with a lively interest in reality, a surprising alertness for happenings in the world around him. This trait became more pronounced as the boy grew up; it saved

22

him from the snares of living in a world of sheer imagination. The power of fairy-tale imaginings gave way to a healthy interest in nature. The being of reality grew up shoulder to shoulder with the being of imagination.

At thirteen or fourteen Janne was already a good shot, beating all his companions in the art of shooting a blackcock on the wing — surely a measure of skill that cannot be combined with a solely passive dreaming disposition.

" Up to fifteen," Sibelius admits jokingly, " I was a great Nimrod. I could spend days on end wandering through field and forest."

But shooting was not his only form of contact with nature. "As you approached Annila," says von Konow, " you could be certain of coming across Janne, a tall, slender boy, wandering about in the neighborhood with a butterfly net in his hand and a tin for plants strapped to his back. Janne's collection of plants was the best in our class at school. The study of nature in every form was his main interest during the early years of his boyhood. On the other hand, to boys' ordinary games, such as ball games, running races, and wrestling, he was indifferent."

A lad of young Jean Sibelius's character could not have been an ideal pupil at school. Von Konow's evi-

23

dence leaves no doubt of his having left much to be desired in this respect:

" Janne found it difficult to sit still during lessons and listen to things that did not interest him in the least. He sat buried in thought and would be quite absent-minded when questioned suddenly. On such occasions our beloved headmaster, Gabriel Geitlin, would look at him reproachfully and say with a deep sigh: ' Good gracious, Sibelius is in another world again! ' A sigh from Geitlin was considered worse than a bad mark.

" But if Janne was called up to the blackboard during a lesson in mathematics, he was obliged, willy-nilly, to collect his thoughts, and then he did excellently. His gift for mathematics was undoubted and he also excelled in the natural-history lessons. He was a great favorite of our teacher of botany and zoology, Otto Collin, never to be forgotten by the boys of Tavastehus, although he often made unrestrained fun of the old man and roused him temporarily to anger. At such times Janne brought out all the humor he was capable of. It is impossible to describe how Janne joked with Collin, it had to be seen. I am sure none of Janne's class-mates can forget how extraordinarily funny he could be.

" Preparation for lessons had little attraction for him. But apart from lessons he read any amount. Not only books for boys, but good authors, and when he was a little older, he developed a keen interest in historical works and descriptions, especially those dealing with the period of King Gustav III and the war with Russia in 1808."

III

THE POWER OF

MUSIC

Janne starts learning the violin seriously — The three children — Janne teaches himself theory — Fresh musical influences — Nature as the young composer's teacher — Matriculation.

T is a healthy boy, not an infant prodigy, that we saw grow up — a boy who spent his happiest hours in close converse with nature. He was distinguished among his companions by an early-developed sense of feeling and imagination, but his main interests were on the whole within the limits of a normal boy's harmonious development.

His musical gifts grew steadily during this process of development, though in harmonious association with his other inclinations. They did not take the form of an obsession that might have led him to an unhealthy attitude towards life at a delicate stage of develop-

26

ment — the constant risk for every musical infant prodigy. Jean Sibelius grew up in an unusually musical environment, and he was certainly an unusually musical
boy, whose talents could have afforded a sharp-sighted
observer safe ground for prophesying for the future.
But there was nothing hectic, excited, or forced about
his musical development.

The all-pervading passion for music that was to decide his choice of a career in good time with irresistible
urgency, broke out with the delivering force of a spring
flood let loose. It was not aroused artificially, but was
the last link in a long subconscious process, not an artificial hothouse product, but a work of nature's own
doing.

Sibelius relates the following about his musical
awakening:

" As I approached the age of fifteen, music took hold
of me with a power that soon set aside my other interests. I then began to take violin lessons in earnest of
the best musician my native town could produce, Gustaf Levander, the conductor of the military band. The
violin carried me away entirely; the wish to become a
great violinist was to be my greatest desire, my proudest
ambition, for the next ten years."

Janne was soon able to appear as a violinist at school
festivals and on other occasions. In spite of his skill,
he suffered, according to von Konow's statement, from

27

a surprising want of confidence. Before every appearance, even if it was only among his companions, he was
tortured by such stage fright that he had to be led to
the platform almost by force. Once he had started
playing, all was well.

When, thanks to methodical teaching, his skill in
playing the violin had increased, Janne was able to devote himself to a form of music that proved of para-
mount importance for his musical training and taste.
His brother and sister had made good progress in
music, too. There was now a complete trio in the
home. His sister Linda played the piano, his brother
Christian the violoncello, and with Janne as the violinist and lively leader of the whole ensemble the brothers and sister began to play chamber music. Outside
his home Janne played in quartets in families in which
chamber music was encouraged, at the homes of Dr.
Theodor Tigerstedt, Major Schulman, and Mr. Elfs-
berg, the chemist.

" Our family trio played classical music almost exclusively, the works of Haydn, Mozart, and Beethoven.
By this means my taste was developed from the very
first in a very strict direction. I still remember that
during the first year of our playing together we came
across a work of Mendelssohn's — I think it was a sonata for violin and piano in F minor. I was so thoroughly impregnated with the classical spirit that I

could not bear the piece. Later, however, we also
played pieces of the romantic school, Schubert, Weber,
and Mendelssohn."

Playing in the family trio encouraged Janne's own
creative vein. His acquaintance with the classics
tempted him to know more of music and its laws. A
fortunate discovery afforded him a good opportunity
of extending his theoretical knowledge; in the autumn
of 1881 he came across Marx's celebrated theory of
composition in the school library. He eagerly devoured
the book and began to learn the theory of music by
himself, which soon gave him a considerable insight
into the construction of the classic masterpieces. He
acquired such extensive knowledge of forms that,
according to his own evidence, he had practically
nothing new to learn in this respect when he began to study music seriously in Helsingfors five years
later.

Encouraged by example and possessed with the desire to apply his newly acquired theoretical knowledge
productively, Janne began to compose for the family
trio. An imposing number of attempts at chamber music saw the light of day in 1881–2, including a trio in
A minor and a piano quartet in E minor. Fragments
have been preserved, showing Sibelius's level at that
time. His compositions are mostly in the classical style.
They have not yet any original musical expression of

their own, but exhibit a respectable mastery of form and attempts at a polyphonic style.

It was of much importance for the musical development of the youth that at that time music in Tavastehus experienced a considerable rise. The musical academy established in Helsingfors in the autumn of 1882 contributed very much to this, its ensemble, composed of good foreign performers, frequently visiting the little town on Lake Vanajavesi and affording its grateful inhabitants an opportunity of hearing chamber music and solos performed with such artistic earnestness and technical accomplishment as surpassed most of what the people of Tavastehus had ever heard. It was of special significance that the visitors from the capital included many of the most valuable new musical works in their programs; in this way Sibelius became acquainted with Grieg's sonatas, the healthy northern realism of which opened his eyes to new musical forms of expression. The growing reputation of Tavastehus as a musical town attracted more and more foreign celebrities. As a youth of eighteen Sibelius heard the 'cellist Carl Davidoff and the pianist Wasilij Safonoff, and during his last term at school such world-wide celebrities as August Wilhelmij and Sophie Menter visited Tavastehus.

Young Sibelius's own compositions reflect the development he passed through during these years. A cycle of tunes for violin and piano, rather misleadingly entitled a sonata, displays, in addition to greater technical skill, lyrical inspiration, born of the sunshine-cult of the northern summer, realism in musical diction, indicating the influence of Grieg to some extent, but at the same time an originality, gushing forth from new sources in the soul of the young composer. The " sonata " probably dates from 1883; in the following year an andantino for violoncello and piano appeared, a precursor of later works as regards construction of melody and harmony. The great miracle had occurred: within a couple of years the youth had developed from a devoted imitator of the classics into a composer capable of expressing himself in a musical language that he could call his own.

The creative vein had been developed in close contact with nature under fruitful reciprocal action between love of nature and musical inspiration that guaranteed the freshness and originality of the result. Young Sibelius's most important compositions during these years, no doubt, resounded as improvisations in the open air.

" I loved to take my violin with me on my summer rambles, so that, whenever I felt inspired, I could express it in music. During the summers in Sääksmäki I selected a platform, for preference, consisting of a stone in Kalalahti with an enchanting view across Vanajavesi.

There I gave the birds endless concerts. The neighborhood of Lovisa inspired me quite as much. When sailing I often stood in the bow with my violin and improvised to the sea."

Nature played on a rich register in the soul of the youth. It absorbed and worked up a variegated series of moods and sensations, which it reproduced in sound varying from profound devotion to playful realism. No experience in nature was too insignificant to be worked up by this constantly wakeful receptivity. It found adequate musical expression for everything.

Von Konow's narrative gives many convincing proofs of the inner connection between experiences in nature and musical invention. A couple of episodes illustrate what varied impressions the young composer could use productively.

" One evening in August," says von Konow, " we came to a shore where flax and hemp, lately taken out of the water, were drying. The hemp gave off a peculiar disgusting smell. Janne noticed the smell, stopped, looked at the ground, and frowned, looking as though he had encountered a phenomenon whose secret he had to discover. For a time he said nothing. Suddenly the strained expression of his features relaxed, he began to hum, and before I knew where I was, we were on our way home. Janne immediately sat down at the piano, started improvising, and soon the sensations evoked by the peculiar smell of the hemp took on a musical form in a grotesque capriccio.

" One sunny Easter Day we walked on the ice that was beginning to melt. We walked for some time, the sun shone brightly, the pools of water on the ice kept growing, and we got our feet wet. But Janne was delighted. ' How lovely it is,' he exclaimed, ' to feel the moisture of the melting ice! ' Soon his imagination was at full stretch. ' Spring is coming, spring is coming,' he cried, and we hurried home to the piano, where the approaching spring slid across the keys in joyful tones."

From the time he was fifteen, Sibelius had devoted himself to music with ever growing passion. It is obvious that this did not benefit his studies at school.

" If I am asked," Sibelius confesses, " what interested me most at school, I can say with a clear conscience: nothing. I must, however, make an exception in favor of natural science, which coincided with my love of nature. History was able to engross my attention at times if it dealt with periods that appealed to my imagination; then I read the dry school-book as though it were a novel. My passion for Ossian's romantic ancient world in my youth I must also, I suppose, ascribe to my interest in history. I must also not forget the classical languages, which opened up a new exalted world of beauty: Homer and Horace had a significance in my development that I cannot value highly enough. Outside music, literature interested me most. I remained true to the poets of my childhood, but I was also seized with interest in modern tendencies in Scandinavian literature. Björnson and Strindberg appeared on my horizon during my last years at school. My better knowledge of the works of the young literature in the Finnish language dates from a later stage."

Although he took very little interest in it, the school curriculum had to be completed. Matriculation was considered at that time in Finland, as it is now, as an indispensable duty of the sons of educated families, and Sibelius's nearest relations were horrified by the prospect of his giving up his studies. Here Sibelius's clear brain made up for lack of interest. His constant violin-playing forced him, on the doctor's advice, to remain for a second year in the fifth form. After that he passed from form to form according to schedule and matriculated on May 15, 1885.

The passion for music accompanied Sibelius the schoolboy and distracted him to the last. A month after being solemnly admitted to the university he was able to write the last notes in the score of a string quartet in E flat major. This last composition during his schooldays revealed technical knowledge and a mastery of form that are striking in a musical adept, who had no teacher but himself.

IV

HELSINGFORS

*Jean Sibelius the student of law — Special student at
the musical academy — Legal studies abandoned —
Dreams of virtuosity — An eccentric musical adept
— Contemporary light on young Sibelius.*

IT was not an entirely happy, emancipated youth
who tramped the streets of Helsingfors in the
autumn of 1885. The young student from Tavastehus
had, indeed, escaped from the restraint of school and
the study of a mass of subjects that did not interest him
in the least. But it had not yet been vouchsafed to
him to follow his most cherished aim. He was forced
to struggle with the consequences of the step he had
taken when on the 30th of May he had been enrolled
at the university as a student of the faculty of law.

Enrolment at the university had been a tribute to
the spirit of the time, personified by a relative whose
wishes the young man considered himself bound to
respect.

" My maternal grandmother," says Sibelius, " would not have approved by any means had I chosen such a risky and disreputable career as that of a musician. It is true she appreciated my artistic gifts and thoroughly approved of my efforts at composing, but the mere thought of music as an occupation seemed an abomination to her. She was old-fashioned and had spent her life in the country and in the provincial town and looked upon a musician as on the same level as a wandering organ-grinder, or not far removed from it. In view of what she had meant to my mother and to us children since my father's death I naturally did all I could to avoid causing her disappointment."

That Sibelius had decided in favor of law was dictated so little by irresistible attraction to that science that he could only reply to the tactless questions of his joking comrades as to the reason for his choice by saying: " What else am I to study? " We should, perhaps, not be far wrong in supposing that Sibelius's choice was due to the circumstance that legal studies formed the preparation as a matter of course for an official career, which was considered in the conservative environment from which he came to be the most honorable for a young man of good family who was anxious to make his way.

By entering the university Sibelius considered that he had fulfilled all the reasonable demands of his family. He did not feel in duty bound to forswear all his musical interests. On September 15, 1885 he was enrolled as a special pupil at the musical academy, where he received instruction in violin-playing and the theory of music. We need not ask whether music or law interested him most. Nor was it long before he was released from the laborious legal studies that agreed so ill with his temperament. He himself tells of an event that contributed actively to this fortunate change in his fate.

" I had borrowed Norman's text-book of Nordic history, which was part of the prescribed course in my time, from a friend. I had not got very far when I put it aside, though with the intention of taking it up again at a time of greater inspiration, for I left it on the window-sill open at the place where I had stopped reading. However, I forgot my good resolution. The book was left lying untouched month after month, exposed to the rays of the sun, with the result that the open pages became quite yellow.

" One day a maternal uncle of mine — I had three, all of them teachers in the provinces — came to town and called on me without warning to inquire about how I was getting on. He happened to go to the window and caught sight of the open book with its yellow pages, which furnished eloquent proof that it had not been in use for a long time. The sight led him to a conclusion

37

about my studies in general and he refrained from discussing the matter any further with these words of resignation:

" ' After all, Janne, it would be best for you to devote yourself entirely to music, seeing that study does not interest you any more than this.' "

It is probably due to the influence of this wise kinsman in the family circle that the young man did not encounter more serious opposition when, after two terms and after passing a preliminary examination, he took his courage in both hands and announced his intention of defying the verdict of society and becoming a musician.

On returning to Helsingfors in September 1886 Jean Sibelius was therefore able to devote himself entirely to his great love, music. He continued along the lines he had started on a year before and divided his interest between playing the violin and working out his theoretical problems at his writing-table. Strange to say, it was the violin that formed the greater attraction for him.

" Everyone has his life's tragedy," says Sibelius jokingly as he looks back upon this period of his life. " Mine was that I wanted to be a celebrated violinist at any price. From the time I was fifteen I played my violin for ten years practically from morning till night. I hated pen and ink and infinitely preferred an elegant violin bow. My preference for the violin lasted quite

long, and it was a very painful awakening when I had
to admit that I had begun my training for the exacting
career of an eminent performer too late. I was at the
age when we chase chimeras and put off as long as possible looking at reality as it is."

During his first years in Helsingfors the young musician devoted himself to the study of musical theory
merely as a complement to his study of the violin. And
he made such progress under the tuition of a gifted
teacher, the temperamental Hungarian, H. Csillag,
that in 1887, though he was only a pupil, he was ap-
pointed as second violinist in the string quartet of the
musical academy, composed of teachers. As the consciousness of the creative forces within him grew, pro-
founder theoretical knowledge became a matter of ever
greater consequence to him, although the dreams of
becoming an eminent player captivated the young man
throughout almost the whole of the '80's.

It was a person of the rarest talent whose training
had been entrusted to the musical academy — a genius
in the making, as original in personality as in gifts, who
fascinated and at the same time puzzled those around
him.

We know how the young musical student appeared
to his intimate friends from Adolf Paul, later a prominent author, who was two years his senior and at that
time still dreamed of becoming a great pianist. He was

in daily intercourse with Sibelius. In his first book, a youthful confession, *A Book about a Man*, Adolf Paul has drawn a portrait of his friend during their years of study. In some points it is obviously a caricature, but in other and more essential parts it possesses decided life and truth.

It is certainly no everyday creature that we find in Adolf Paul's character sketch:

" He always gave the impression of having suddenly dropped from a distant planet or of having made his entry into this world in some other impossible way, for everything endowed his imagination with the most peculiar qualities, nothing could proceed naturally. His imaginative powers were always searching for the most out-of-the-way, unfathomable causes of every event. And to make combinations between the most incompatible things was the simplest and most natural thing in the world to him.

" Ideas came to him glimmering on a ray of sunshine reflected in the water — falling with a dead leaf — hopping like a bird — yes, even an ordinary, simple shower of rain, such as can come down anywhere you like in the countryside and run off in the shape of dirty, muddy water into the nearest ditch, made ideas crop up in his brain like mushrooms on damp ground.

" And what ideas they were!

" Just as there was no connection between mush-

40

rooms and the rain that had forced them out of their dark nothingness, so there was as little connection between his ideas and the outer causes that made them see the light of day.

" These outer causes were only so many jolts that set all the wonderful machinery in his brain in action — merely motive power, necessary, of course, but of no further significance to the resulting product. He was a real natural genius, thoroughly individual, without the slightest relationship to others."

And then a description of how inspiration worked in this eccentric natural genius:

" The moods that made an impression on him were identified in his brain with some shade of color, and then, only when the mood and tone of color were distinct, the actual work of composition began. Then the motif, the correct rhythms and correct harmonies placed themselves readily at his service.

" To run about and find good, original motifs and then go home to a studio, decorated in Chinese fashion, and there, according to all the rules of art and without transgressing any philosophical system, turn out something that no one had ever done before was a method of composing that he did not even despise, because he knew nothing about it.

" For him there existed a strange, mysterious connection between sound and color, between the most secret perceptions of eye and ear. Everything he saw produced a corresponding impression on his ear — every impression of sound was transferred and fixed as color on the retina of his eye and thence to his memory. And this he thought natural, with as good reason as those who did not possess this faculty called him crazy or affectedly original.

" For this reason he only spoke of this in the strictest confidence and under a pledge of silence. ' For otherwise they will make fun of me! ' "

The same impression of something puzzling and confusing, of a creature that was not bound by the same laws as ordinary people, was made by young Sibelius on a representative of a slightly older generation, and a very critical observer, who already had extensive experience of individuals and types. Karl Flodin was a man of undoubted reputation as a critic and writer when a friend invited him to a café to meet a young man, quite unknown to the public, it is true, but nevertheless such a peculiar person that it was worth while making his acquaintance. The meeting took place in Forsström's café, a restaurant recently opened in the center of Helsingfors.

" The acquaintance was established in a moment," Flodin relates, " and eternal fraternity drunk, if I remember rightly. Sibelius was the name of my new brother, Jean Sibelius, a student and a man of Nyland, like ourselves. He played the violin and was a pupil at the musical academy.

" There was something peculiarly fascinating about his slender figure. It was as if his straightforward nature always wanted to meet one with open arms. But you were never sure whether there was not, after all, some mockery behind it. His speech overflowed with paradoxes and metaphors, without allowing you to realize what was serious and what only played on the surface like bubbles born of odd caprices in his quick brain.

" His fair hair fell untidily in wisps across his brow. His eyes gazed as if through a dull mist, but when his imagination began to play restlessly, his look became deeper and glittered with a blue brilliancy. His ears were also remarkable, large, well-shaped catchers of sound, the ears of a musician, such as Beethoven may have had. . . .

" Our conversation darted about like a hare in the undergrowth. Before we knew where we were, Sibelius was juggling with colors and sounds as if they were bright glass balls, made colors resound and sounds glow, so that A major became blue and C major red, F major green and D major yellow, or something like that, and everything in the world had its own melodious label, every mood of nature its ready-coined motif, every sensation its primeval chord, as if you could preserve the sound-bodies in small boxes and take them out for use when required. Little did we suspect then that a creative force was already breathing within this youth, that the canvas for a new world-picture was already being raised out of these visions and fantasies, however confused they now seemed to us, however little firm foundation and connection they seemed to possess.

" I cannot remember how our meeting ended. But the portrait of Jean Sibelius had burned itself into my mind, I was all attention when his name was mentioned, and when his friends in the musical academy were surprised by his first bold compositions in chamber music, in which seething inspiration battled bravely with established forms and means of expression, which he wanted to fill with his young wine — then I saw him again before me as he appeared the first time, plunging head-first into a sea of foaming ideas."

This was the uncurbed young genius whose seething vitality the musical academy was to guide into law-bound, productive furrows, whose revolutionary disposition was to be made to develop its full possibilities by means of strict schooling. It was a difficult task. It demanded a teacher with sufficient authority to make a revolutionary talent spend hour after hour at the desk, dutifully performing the often uninspiring tasks of theoretical training, and at the same time sufficient of a

psychologist to be able to interpret his pupil's originality and to understand how to gain his confidence and
affection.

The musical academy possessed such a teacher in the
person of its head, Martin Wegelius, in whom both
qualities were united in a rarely happy combination.

V

A PUPIL AT THE

MUSICAL ACADEMY

*Martin Wegelius — Master and pupil — The double
life of a budding composer — First appearance as a
composer — End of the years of study in Finland.*

ARTIN WEGELIUS was at this time at the height
of his vigor. Forty years of age, he devoted all
his energies to the institution that he had brought into
being with great effort four years earlier. A person of
culture, who would have made his mark in any part of
the world, he was a rarity in the Finland of the '80's,
particularly in its musical life. His devotion to his task,
his self-sacrificing idealism, his eloquent preaching of
the necessity of a liberal humanistic education for a
professional musician, his whole personality, were calculated to captivate a pupil who, extremely quick to
discover human failings and limitations in spite of all
his enthusiasm and warmheartedness, would have

found it hard to reconcile himself to a dry pedant. "Martin Wegelius," Sibelius testifies, "was, if anyone, the right man in the right place. He devoted himself with passion to his calling as a teacher. He lived entirely for the musical academy and knew how to infect teachers and pupils with his love of work and his burning enthusiasm. During my subsequent travels for purposes of study I was able to convince myself that the musical academy, thanks to Martin's personal influence, was on a considerably higher level than most of such institutions abroad."

With intuitive perception Wegelius recognized his pupil's unusual talent. He realized what treasures were hidden here and felt his responsibility all the more. The more original and revolutionary the pupil's gifts were, the more anxious he was to give them a firm basis in a thorough theoretical foundation. He applied his efforts to teach his pupil, methodically and at not too hurried a pace, all the knowledge that appertained to the technical equipment of a genuine musician, starting from general musical instruction and harmony and going on to strict and free polyphonic style and the knowledge of forms according to the classical scheme. The program and pace tried the pupil's patience at times, but the preservation of their trustful personal contact was ensured on the one hand by the teacher's unswerving interest, on the other by the pupil's feeling

47

that the severe demands were dictated by broad-minded goodwill. Martin Wegelius and Jean Sibelius, almost twenty years younger, became very close friends.

" Martin Wegelius was always a fatherly friend to me," his pupil recalls gratefully almost half a century later. " His interest in me was not confined to what I did as a pupil within the walls of the musical academy, but extended much further. This was all the more re-markable seeing that, with his neo-romantic tendency, he could not agree with me on all points, though before strangers he always sang my praises.

" In the summer I spent many weeks, sometimes months, at his invitation in his summer home on Gran-holmen (Fir Island) in the western archipelago near Helsingfors. Those summers were of extraordinary value to me. In the mornings I worked assiduously at counterpoint. In the afternoons we played sonatas — principally classic ones. I played the violin and Mar-tin, who was a trained pianist, took the piano part. The day usually ended in cosy conclave round a tray of cooling drinks. Wegelius read aloud to us, while his wife, Hanna, a wonderful woman, performed her duties as hostess. As a rule Martin preferred literary works and books on the history of civilization. Many eve-nings, for instance, were devoted to Gobineau's book on the *Renaissance*, which Martin translated, as he read, from the original French, but so fluently, without

A PUPIL AT THE MUSICAL ACADEMY

stumbling or pausing, that one could not believe that
he was not reading a Swedish translation."

Martin Wegelius was a convinced adherent of the
neo-German school, in which Richard Wagner, after
the great classics, represented the highest point and
the one thing necessary to salvation in the sphere of
music.

" This attitude," Sibelius declares, " dictated Martin's principles, too, when he was engaged in familiariz-
ing his pupils with contemporary music. He acted very
personally on this point. Brahms, for instance, was
scarcely played at all at the concerts and musical evenings of the musical academy. As he was Wagner's
rival, Martin took little notice of him."

With the best will in the world, Sibelius found it difficult to imbibe his teacher's ideas of what was valuable
and first-class in modern music. Wegelius tried in vain
to infect him with his admiration for Wagner; neither
then nor later, in spite of a pilgrimage to Bayreuth, the
holy shrine of all faithful Wagnerians, did Wagner play
any part for Sibelius. As a young musical student Sibelius was attracted more by composers of a more realistic, purely musical character. Among those who
made an impression on him at that time was, above all,
Grieg, Tchaikovsky being, perhaps, second; if we try
to detect external influences in the compositions in
which he confessed his young soul during his first years

49

in Helsingfors, our thoughts are constantly led to the northern master. Neither Grieg nor Tchaikovsky enjoyed Wegelius's favor to any great extent. When Sibelius played Tchaikovsky's *Sérénade mélancolique*, accompanied by his master, one evening at Granholmen, the latter's comment was laconic, but expressive: " For the violin, rubbish! "

These diverging tastes did not diminish Martin Wegelius's interest in young Sibelius. He was far from endeavoring in earnest to discourage his originality; he would not have succeeded, and such violation of another person's individuality would, besides, have been foreign to Wegelius's nature. But on one point he was adamant: as a teacher he demanded that his pupils, so long as they were his responsibility, should follow blindly the scheme he had drawn up for their theoretical training.

" Martin was an extraordinarily interesting teacher," Sibelius says, " but at the same time an authoritative nature, extremely anxious that his pupil should carry out the program marked out for him. He was often really angry if his instructions were not obeyed in all points."

Sibelius was therefore obliged, especially during the first stages of his studies with Wegelius, to live a double life. As a pupil at the musical academy he had to fulfill conscientiously the tasks his teacher set him — and

Sibelius took trouble to do so, realizing the advantage of the knowledge he was being given. If he wanted to find an outlet for his feelings as a composer in the making, he had to do so independently of his tasks of study.

It is quite intelligible that under such circumstances the most remarkable works of Sibelius during his first years in Helsingfors were composed, so to say, in secret, long before he appeared in public as the academy's most promising pupil in composition. The F major sonata for violin and piano, permeated by fresh natural inspiration, composed in the winter of 1886–7, revealed in its independent treatment of forms and in its bold harmonies little of the pupil under the rod of a severe master, forced to move within the limits of prescribed rules of art. The sonata had a closely related successor in a piano trio, written in the summer of 1887 in Korpo, where Sibelius lived with his mother and his brother and sister in a little house close to the mansion of Korpo, an old country seat dating from the time of Sweden's era of greatness.

These, and some minor compositions that saw the light of day outside the musical academy, were only known to a very small circle. " I advanced slowly along my own line," says Sibelius. " I guarded my double life jealously, so that exceedingly few got to know of the works in which I expressed my innermost strivings."

51

Knowing young Sibelius's frank nature, we may feel sure that this double life was not unknown to Martin Wegelius. And the fact that in the spring of 1888 he asked his gifted pupil to collaborate in composing the music to Gunnar Wennerberg's dramatic fairy-tale, *The Watersprite*, that was to be performed at a dramatic and musical evening arranged by the musical academy, proves undoubtedly that the severe master did not take a harsh view of it. Wegelius wrote most of the music himself, but entrusted the central part, the Watersprite's song, repeated three times in varied form, to Sibelius.

Sibelius's contribution to *The Watersprite* was of no considerable extent and might have been omitted from our narrative if the performance of the play, on April 9, 1888, had not been a red-letter day in the life of the composer, as it was then that he appeared for the first time as a composer before a larger audience than the teachers of the academy and his nearest relations and friends.

At about the same time as "The Watersprite's Song," another work appeared that was a considerably better indication of its author's future career, *Nights of Jealousy* — a work describing personal experience throughout, full of intense feeling and lyrical beauty.

"*Nights of Jealousy*," Sibelius declares, "belongs

SIBELIUS AS A MUSICAL STUDENT, 1888

entirely to my romantic period, and has, indeed, very little of Runeberg in it."

A few weeks after the performance of *The Watersprite*, at the pupils' demonstration of the musical academy on May 31, Sibelius publicly produced a more important result of his studies with Wegelius, from an academic point of view, in a Theme and Variations in C sharp minor for string quartet. The composition was intended to be the result of a conscientious pupil's work, the test of an apprentice, and as such it satisfied all reasonable claims; a more personal achievement was rendered impossible by the nature of the task.

Sibelius had now studied with Wegelius for three years and had dutifully carried out his master's strict scheme in the compositions he had worked out under his supervision. Wegelius realized that the time had come to give freer rein to his talented pupil and allow him, even in the works that were included in his regular course of training, to develop his individual style, which had already expressed itself so richly, especially when he composed on his own. The result showed itself in two works with which Sibelius concluded his studies at the musical academy: a string suite in A major for violin, viola, and violoncello, performed on April 13, 1889, and a string quartet in A minor, performed on May 29, 1889.

Both compositions revealed such originality in technique and inventiveness that they struck his contemporaries with admiring astonishment: they realized that they were face to face with something quite novel. All the leaders of musical life in Helsingfors were present as eagerly applauding listeners at this, Sibelius's actual début as a composer, among them Karl Flodin, who was now able to convince himself that his strange acquaintance of Forsström's café was something more than a chatty eccentric who toyed with whims and impulses.

Later on I shall describe how such a congenial artist as Ferruccio Busoni, nurtured in the large European centers of music, was awakened at a stroke to the consciousness that here was a genius of quite unusual degree. I cannot resist the temptation to quote Flodin's opinions in evidence of the first reaction of the severest and most expert Finnish critic of that time to such a phenomenon as Sibelius. Of the five movements of the string suite Flodin thought it safe to assert that " they bore evidence of their composer having studied the musical secrets of the string quartet with intelligent talent and given practical assistance in producing them. The independent counterpoint treatment of the three instruments was also very excellent, even inspired; not excellent in the ordinary scholastic sense, but thoroughly novel and modern. Frankly, I was astonished by the début of this composer."

His opinion of the A minor quartet was equally enthusiastic:

" In this composition M. Sibelius has given such brilliant proof of original musical talent that we may expect the greatest things of him. In all the different movements of the quartet there was a wealth of ideas and independence, combined with mastery of the technical difficulties, that must be described as unique qualities in the case of so young a composer. At one step M. Sibelius has placed himself in the front rank of those to whom it is entrusted to be the standard-bearers of Finnish creative music."

VI

LIFE
IN HELSINGFORS

Helsingfors in the '80's — Albert Edelfelt — Zachris Topelius — Ferruccio Busoni — Introduction to Järnefelt's family — The last summer in Lovisa before going abroad.

SIBELIUS's first years in Helsingfors were not passed solely in playing the violin and studying composition under the strict supervision of Martin Wegelius. His alert receptiveness to the outer world that showed itself during his schooldays in his love of nature and of life in field and forest found fresh forms of expression in some respects. A new world of reality had opened up to the young man, a new environment with new people and new problems.

"Helsingfors was a country town in the '80's," Sibelius relates. "The population was small, everyone was acquainted. No political clouds darkened the

56

horizon, money did not play the same part in society as it does now, and people enjoyed themselves thoroughly. Great feasts were held that lasted two or three days at a stretch. If often happened that I was called on by committees who begged me to compose something for this or that occasion. I always used to accede to their request and consequently composed a good deal of incidental festive music.

"Life was mostly looked at through rose-colored spectacles. Hours of despondency passed rapidly when you were with your companions discussing ambitious plans for the future, most frequently in the small taverns that were the favorite resort of youth at that time, or sometimes, when in a more festive mood and purses were better lined, in one of the larger restaurants.

"Life in the latter presented a different picture from what it does in our day. You seldom saw such full houses as now; as a rule the dining-rooms were sparsely occupied. This was due to the strict control exercised at the door. Only a select public was allowed in, and therefore — a thing that is impossible at present — you could see decently dressed and respectable people refused admittance. It was the same at the numerous fancy-dress balls: there was very strict control of those trying to gain admittance."

A young musical student who did not push himself forward and preferred the society of his intimates

rather than public occasions did not come into touch
with celebrities in Helsingfors in those days. There
were, however, a couple of exceptions.

"One day towards the end of the '80's I became
acquainted by chance with our great painter Albert
Edelfelt at Kämp's. He began to talk of my father at
once, whom he had seen as a boy in his parents' house
in Tavastehus, and said that he remembered his appearance so well that he could have drawn him at a
moment's notice. Recollections of the town where we
had both spent our childhood created a friendly atmosphere from the first between Edelfelt and myself, but
there could be no question of a closer intimacy between us. Edelfelt was more than ten years my senior
and already an acknowledged master in his sphere, I
was only a promising young man. We became friends
only later, in the '90's, but I cannot claim that our
friendship was ever intimate. The difference in age,
especially as it was not made up for by common interest
in our work, meant ever so much more in my youth
than it does today."

Young Sibelius's first meeting with Zachris Topelius,
the great romantic author and former Principal of
Helsingfors University, was not nearly so happy.

"Topelius was once invited by Martin Wegelius to
the hospitable house of the head of the musical acad-

emy in Helsingfors. Wegelius introduced me to Topelius as a promising young composer, whereupon the
kind old man asked me to play one of my compositions
to him. On Wegelius' advice I decided to play my
romance for the violin in B minor.

"Wegelius sat down at the piano, and I was preparing to draw my bow across the strings, when I saw
through the open door that the next room was full
of young girls anxious to view the event at close quarters. I was not interested in this additional audience,
I wanted to play to Topelius alone, so I went and
closed the door. Topelius, however, was delighted to
see young faces, and when I returned to my place I
noticed that he was not at all pleased by my behavior.

"I dropped still lower in his estimation later in the
evening when we spoke of contemporary literature.
Mention was made of Strindberg, whose books Topelius despisingly called 'mere dung,' while I could
not repress my admiration for *The Red Room*. The
old man must have thought that I was tainted with
the same disrespectful spirit as the despised Strindberg, for after this I saw clearly that he could not really
get on with me. He was not fair to me, for I was the
most devoted admirer he could have wished for."

Sibelius spent his time in the '80's principally with
the friends he made at the musical academy. He took

no part in academic life and in the discussions of the nationality question, which were very heated at the time.

At the musical institute Sibelius became acquainted with a young foreigner of whom we have caught glimpses in our narrative, and who had already made a name for himself in the realm of European music, Ferruccio Busoni. This German-Italian, of about the same age as Sibelius, fascinating both as a musician and as an individual, was engaged as a piano teacher at the musical academy at this stage of his meteoric career, in 1888–90, the most brilliant of the remarkable talented foreigners whom Wegelius had succeeded in attracting to his small academy in Helsingfors. A close friendship grew up between the inspired teacher, a rara avis in that climate, and the student of composition, also an uncommon phenomenon.

All honor to Busoni's intuitive perception that he was able immediately to discover Sibelius's originality and appreciate it. It was really the string trio that opened Busoni's eyes to Sibelius's very uncommon gifts. Busoni was to testify to this more than a quarter of a century later, when, while living in Zürich during the war, he performed Sibelius's second symphony in March 1916 and, true to his custom, introduced the composer by a few lines in the papers. " I had the opportunity — in connection with my former residence in Helsingfors — of witnessing the Finnish composer's first attempts at composition. A suite for string trio attracted my attention (and the attention of his clever violin master, Csillag) at that time. We were all attention when we realized that we were confronted with something that was far above the level of a pupil's work."

" My acquaintance with Busoni," says Sibelius, " was most stimulating to me. In one respect we were as unlike each other as possible. Busoni had grown up as an infant prodigy and had spent his youth in hotels in practically every town in Europe. He came in contact with nature for the first time in Finland. In the early stages of our acquaintance he was very much surprised by the great benefits I was able to draw from my communing with nature. Later he understood me better, although with his very intellectual, reflective attitude he could never surrender unreservedly to natural impressions.

"We were on intimate terms from the first. In spite of his being a teacher and I a pupil, we met almost daily. Besides, I was not his pupil, as lessons in piano-playing did not form part of my curriculum at the musical academy; we were drawn together by our common musical interests in general. Our usual meeting-place was Ericson's café, very popular at that time, where Armas Järnefelt, my future brother-in-law, and

Adolf Paul, both of them Busoni's pupils, also used to turn up regularly. When Busoni was in the humor for it, and that happened pretty often, he invited the three of us to supper at Kämp's. His was a generous nature, cordial and impulsive. He played a good deal to us during our meetings, either the works of his favorite composers or improvisations of his own. He encouraged us, too, to improvise to him, and I readily took advantage of his indulgence to defects in my skill on the piano. When there was no music, Busoni kept up our spirits by relating his experiences in various countries, described with infectious animation and interlarded with excellent character sketches and jokes. He was unsurpassed as a punster.

" He displayed an interest in my music that both pleased and flattered me. He looked forward eagerly to my A minor quartet, my last composition at the musical academy, and when I had completed it and showed him the score, he seated himself at once at the piano and played through the whole quartet from beginning to end without previously having had an opportunity of glancing at the music. And how he played it! "

Busoni's interest in Sibelius's music was not of a transient kind nor dictated by a desire to make himself popular in the place where his work happened to lie for the time being. It grew as time went by. It was only after 1900, when Busoni started the famous series of orchestral concerts in Berlin that were to mean so much to the success of modern music, that Sibelius realized how strong the bonds of friendship were for the world-famous musician, too, that had been established between the two young men in Helsingfors.

" Busoni's friendship," Sibelius testifies gratefully, " was in general of the kind that expresses itself more in deeds than in words. We often met later, on the last occasion in 1921 at a concert in London, where he played his *Indian Fantasy* and I conducted my fourth symphony. Busoni's premature death in 1924 was a heavy blow to me."

" Towards the end of the '80's I was introduced to the Järnefelt family. Lieutenant-General Järnefelt, who subsequently became my father-in-law, was an uncommon man in many respects, a character of unusual quality, who made a career in the Russian Empire under difficult circumstances, but nevertheless ever preserved a great love for his fatherland and formed a very independent opinion regarding our internal affairs. His wife, Elisabeth, née Baroness Clodt von Jürgensburg, came of a Baltic family with a keen love of art. Husband and wife formed a great contrast. He was grave, haughtily reserved, a thorough aristocrat in his zeal for the Finnish people, an official and soldier — she lively, friendly, liberal-minded, full of sympathy for the

63

lower classes not only in principle, but also in practice, devoted to literature and art. The introduction to this family was of the greatest significance to me. It represented a form of culture that was quite new to me — a breath of air from Europe. A very unusual family — you could not tell whether the military or artistic aspect predominated. Three sons of the family were destined for artistic work. Arvid was still busy completing his legal studies, but was soon to abandon all his plans for an official career to devote himself to authorship and his ideals. The two younger ones, Eero and Armas, had already sworn allegiance to art. The strange part was that their father, a man thoroughly devoted to duty and earnestness, although he had dreamed of a different future for his sons, never attempted, when the time came, to enforce his authority in order to influence them against their will in the choice of a career."

The acquaintance with the Järnefelt family was of great significance for the future shaping of Sibelius's fate. Theirs was one of the few homes at that time where convinced Finnish nationalistic sympathies were combined with inherited refinement. Here Sibelius had an opportunity of coming into contact with young Finnish currents of culture that had hitherto been foreign to the young man brought up in a Swedish environment. In this circle, too, he found his life's partner.

Having completed his studies at the musical academy, Jean Sibelius went, as so often before, with his mother, sister and brother to Lovisa to regain strength and inspiration in the hospitable home of his aunt. The summer passed as before in playing music with his brother and sister and in composing industriously.

An eyewitness of those days has drawn a portrait that gives us a lifelike idea of Jean Sibelius in his youth. This eyewitness is Alma Söderhjelm, a well-known Swedo-Finnish woman historian who lived in Lovisa at the same time with her father and some girl friends. She writes of the Sibelius brothers in *My World:*

" Kitti (Christian) was twenty-one and had recently taken his degree as Bachelor of Philosophy and had done so well in all the subjects that every one of his instructors — as one of his friends told me — was anxious that he should ' continue in his particular subject.' . . . Kitti was to become a doctor. . . . He was healthy as the morning breeze, freshness and gaiety surrounded him wherever he went, jolly and downright, manly and young; even in his voice there was something exciting. . . . He had a brilliant intellect, a character of gold; neither Linda, his mother, nor his aunt had any worries about him. . . .

" Janne was older and was then twenty-three. He was pale and good-looking, slender and sensitive. He was also very absent-minded. His mother told me that when she had a coffee party for ladies that summer and all her guests were seated in the drawing-room with their cups of coffee and cakes, the door opened and Janne came in in a short shirt, seated himself at the piano, and began to play, not noticing that there was anyone in the room. . . .

" He seemed to us all a strange and attractive being. And, of course, we were all in love with him. . . . And he was lovable. Refined, attractive, polite, he had that something that women must love. And he was so far above the rest of us. He spoke in such an interesting way. He knew so much. He told us of Macbeth and that he thought of writing a symphony on the subject. He seized the book and read long passages to us, then suddenly he ran to the piano and played a few notes to show what it was to sound like. . . . But usually he lost himself there and played and played, anything that came into his head. The drawing-room was an old-fashioned, bright room in a wooden house. His mother was gentle, and she would often sit and shake her head as she sat and listened to him. . . .

" He did not dance himself, for he was unwell and was not allowed to dance. Instead he played dance music in order to do us a favor. It was more interesting than suitable for dancing to. Even at that time Sibelius's music was not really suitable for dancing. It

66

was very good and in strict time when he began, but very soon he would put in trills and runs that were quite out of place. Instead of sitting down and listening and enjoying it, we demanded stubbornly that he should play dance music, and he was obedient and pulled himself together; after every reminder all went well again for a short time. . . ."

It is interesting to hear, for the first time, as far as we know, that at the age of twenty-three Jean Sibelius was thinking of a Macbeth symphony. The plan was not carried out, however, and perhaps he did not mean it very seriously. At the same time, however, it occupied the mind of another young man all the more, one who was a year older than Sibelius and to whom it was granted to express the somber, terrifying tragedy in Shakspere's drama in music. This young man was Richard Strauss, at that time the energetic conductor of the court orchestra in Weimar. His symphonic poem *Macbeth* was produced during the following winter.

The time was not yet ripe for Sibelius to launch out into the gigantic apparatus of the modern orchestra. The fruit of the solitary hours of the twenty-three-year-old youth at his desk, anxiously hidden from the outer world, was a composition in a sphere already tested,

67

where he could now, released from all fetters, move with greater independence than ever before: the string quartet in B flat major, a work in which the young composer's bright joy in creating glows like sunshine on the fresh foliage of the trees — a beautiful, joyful farewell to an epoch in his life, full of endeavor and experience.

VII

IN THE OUTER
WORLD

*Off to Berlin — The German capital in the '80's —
Nothing new produced in music — Albert Becker, an
orthodox master — Hans von Bülow, Richard Strauss,
Joseph Joachim — The quintet in G minor.*

THE SUMMER of 1889, of which he had made good
use, ended the first phase of Jean Sibelius's creative musical development.

Though not yet twenty-four, his output was already
respectable. In regard to external variety and superficially acquired " modernism " it could, of course, not
compete with the achievements of his contemporaries
in the large musical centers of Europe. But as regards
inner spiritual variety, fruitful originality, and latent
power it was far above anything produced by anyone
else in the little country in the far north, and it already
revealed that self-reliance, that independence of cur-

rent fashions, that courage in obeying the laws of his own being, that were in due time to ensure its author an undisputed place in the European music of the twentieth century.

It was time for the young musician to visit the battle-fields on which the great battles in the world of music were fought out.

The financial preparations for his first journey abroad had already been made in the spring, when the student corporation of Nyland had awarded Sibelius a scholar-ship of 1,500 marks (about 290 dollars). With this sum as a basis and the government grant that could be reckoned upon later, Sibelius's journey was more or less assured.

On Saturday, September 7, 1889, Sibelius went on board the steamer *Grand Duke*, ready to start for Lübeck. The young man was full of expectant excite-ment over his first step into the world. He had ac-quaintances on board. His fellow-travelers included Werner Söderhjelm, the young humanist, and his wife, the painter Eero Järnefelt, and the young Finnish nov-elist, Juhani Aho, who was starting like Sibelius on his first journey abroad. Järnefelt and Aho were both bound for Paris; the Söderhjelm family, like Sibelius, was making for Berlin. On the quay stood Martin Wegelius, who called out fatherly admonitions to Si-belius and entrusted him to Werner Söderhjelm's care.

" It was extremely pleasant for me to make the journey with Werner Söderhjelm and his family," says Sibelius. " Söderhjelm was then thirty, already a university tutor and experienced traveler, who guided my stumbling footsteps in the great city with competent knowledge. Our stay together in Berlin laid the foundations of a friendship that was to grow closer as the years went by. In the evening after our arrival in Berlin he took us to the Kroll Opera, where I saw Francesco d'Andrade, then at the beginning of his career act Don Juan as brilliantly as he did a quarter of a century later."

Berlin was, on the threshold of the '90's, in the second year of the reign of Wilhelm II, a city that was expanding enormously, materially and culturally. The regular development during the twenty years since the city had become the capital of the German Empire proceeded with increased speed under the encouraging influence of the personality of a young ruler rich in initiative and keen to experiment, while the stamp of solid power was still maintained, for old Bismarck still had his hand on the rudder of State.

The young man from Finland was not overpowered by his first impressions of the capital of Wilhelm II.

" Berlin looked," Sibelius says, " in spite of its size and its external development of power, in many respects as I had imagined the town in the old Prussian period. Nor did the Germans whom I came across appear in all respects as models from whom I had to learn. I gained the impression that in many respects the educated classes in Finland were considerably more advanced."

The German capital may possibly not have revealed its most interesting features at first sight. The most apparent outward phenomena, military power, material prosperity, North German stiffness, bureaucracy, were, of course, likely to mislead the foreigner. It contributed to Sibelius's disappointment that in the sphere in which he expected fresh inspiration he found nothing but stagnation and sterility.

" There was in general nothing emptier in the realm of music than the transition to the '90's. Nothing new was produced. How different that time was from the time we live in! It is impossible nowadays even to understand the ideas that were in the air. The '80's lived entirely under the influence of imitators of the classics and romantics. The struggle between the partisans of Brahms and Wagner occupied all men's minds. The only young composer who enjoyed undisputed respect in Berlin was August Bungert; he was played a great deal. People seemed to see a new Wagner in him! The times were altogether very pessimistic. And I was anything but a pessimist! "

The struggle between Brahmsians and Wagnerians

SIBELIUS DURING HIS STUDIES IN BERLIN,
1889-90

did not spur Sibelius on to active participation. In his fundamental attitude towards music he preferred Brahms, but he was not his favorite composer, and he saw no reason to alter the attitude of reserve towards Wagner that he had already adopted in Helsingfors, in spite of Wegelius's energetic propaganda, when, during the early part of his stay in Berlin, he heard two of the composer's works, *Die Meistersinger* and *Tannhäuser*, in the theater. He summed up his impressions in a letter to Wegelius dated September 29: " There was such a peculiar mixture of surprise, disappointment, joy within me." The reserve in his opinion is clearly evident, if we remember that these words were addressed to a fanatical Wagnerian and at the same time a friend whose feelings Sibelius was anxious to spare at any price.

Wegelius had given Sibelius a letter of introduction to Albert Becker, greatly respected in his day as a theorist and composer. In this haughty gentleman Sibelius encountered the personification of musical conservatism.

" Albert Becker," thus Sibelius describes his first teacher on foreign soil, " was a robust old fellow of about sixty. He occupied a high position in the musical life of Berlin. He was a director of the cathedral choir and a member of the senate of the Royal Academy of Arts. Becker was a great favorite at court. It was as-

73

serted with conviction that it was he who had written the music for Wilhelm II's *Gesang an Ägir* – ' The Kaiser merely whistled,' people said in Berlin. Becker had been entrusted with the honorable task of writing a funeral march for the burial of the Emperor Frederick. While I was studying with him, the composition appeared in print, and I was able to help him with the proofs."

Martin Wegelius had advised Sibelius to submit in all points to Becker's methods of instruction and " never to contradict him with a look." Sibelius obeyed loyally. He conscientiously analyzed all the motets and fugues of Bach that Becker put before him, solved innumerable problems of composition in strict style, and worked out one vocal fugue after another, so that soon he " knew the German Psalter backwards," as he jokingly expressed it to his fatherly friend in Helsingfors.

" I had private lessons with Becker, which he gave in his home in Hohenzollernstrasse, where he lived in the same house as Ernst von Wildenbruch; I did not know at that time what an important man Wildenbruch was. I wrote fugues in strict style for Becker and other counterpoint. Old Becker was very orthodox on musical subjects. ' *Lieber langweilig, aber im Stil* (Rather dull, but in the strict style) ,' he used to say.

74

" I worked seriously with Becker and put together many fugues, both instrumental and vocal. But I could not resist the feeling that all the time I was dealing with things that belonged to the past, and at times my patience almost failed. I bore it bravely, however, and have not regretted it since. Practice in strict style seems to me today to be as important for a composer as the study of anatomy for a sculptor. Both are equally necessary. You must know your craft. I do not believe that a modern musician can dispense with a methodical training in strict style without its leaving traces in his art."

While Sibelius failed to find much that pointed to the future in the predominating tendencies of taste in Berlin, and while Albert Becker was, perhaps, at that stage not entirely an ideal teacher for him, and while he discovered few direct impulses generally for his own creative faculty, he was able with all the more benefit to listen to the performances provided by executant musicians. On this point Sibelius's testimony is unreserved:

" The greatest importance of my sojourn in Berlin consisted undoubtedly in my being able to hear so much music, both orchestral and chamber music. At home I had had to be content with what was performed at the concerts of the musical academy and in private

75

houses. Here you had the enormously wealthy musical life of an international city, and of the German musical metropolis to boot."

It was only in Berlin that Jean Sibelius had an opportunity of hearing orchestral music on a large scale. A new and copious section of musical literature became accessible to him; he could begin to probe the attractive sound-secrets of the orchestra. This advantage he had had to forgo almost entirely in Helsingfors.

This circumstance may seem so curious to the reader of a later period that it may, perhaps, call for explanation. During the whole time that Sibelius first lived in Helsingfors, the town had had a permanent symphony orchestra, established by Robert Kajanus within a few months of the founding of the musical academy. But the collaboration that should have been so natural between the two undertakings was rendered impossible owing to grave dissensions caused by competition for concert audiences and profound differences in the leaders' views on the requirements of a musical training. The tension was so severe that it was considered most unsuitable for adherents of the musical academy to attend concerts of the orchestra or for members of the orchestra to encourage the efforts of the musical academy. Owing to this bitter feud between the two leading musical institutions of the capital, which only became more reconciled in the middle '90's, Sibelius had only had opportunities now and then, during his studies in Helsingfors, of listening to good orchestral music. In Berlin he was able to make up for this in rich measure.

" The musical life of Berlin, so far as executants are concerned," he tells us, " was governed by those great names Bülow and Joachim. Hans von Bülow was then, a few years prior to his death, at the height of his art. The most unforgettable of all that he presented in his famous series of ' historical piano recitals ' is his rendering of Beethoven's sonatas. I am more than ready to subscribe to what Liszt said of the edition of these works with Bülow's commentaries: that a study of them means more than a dozen musical academies.

" As conductor of the philharmonic concerts, which rapidly became the principal events in the musical life of Berlin thanks to him, Bülow was as supreme as at the piano. I still have old Beethoven scores in my possession in which I made notes according to his interpretations.

" At one of these concerts I heard a work by Richard Strauss for the first time, *Don Juan*, which was still looked upon as a shockingly revolutionary creation. Strauss himself was present at the concert, and his living image remains in my memory as he rose from his seat in the auditorium to acknowledge the applause — a shy young man with a large head of hair. Compared

77

with the works that appeared later, a symphonic poem like *Don Juan* seems almost classically simple and intelligible. When I became acquainted with Strauss more than ten years later, I pointed this out to him. He agreed. His answer was very characteristic: '*Damals hatte ich noch nicht die Geigen geteilt* (At that time I had not yet divided the violins).'

"In this connection," Sibelius continued, "I can quote another instance of the backwardness of the times. Once in the spring of 1890 I traveled with Adolf Paul to Leipzig to meet Ferruccio Busoni, my great friend and Paul's former piano teacher. We attended a concert at which Busoni and the distinguished Brodsky quartet performed Sinding's quintet in F minor. Can you imagine that this easily intelligible work was greeted with hooting? — only a small number in the auditorium dared to applaud. Among the members of the Brodsky quartet I became acquainted on that occasion with some of the distinguished instrumentalists of the day — Brodsky, the violinist, Klengel, the celebrated violoncellist, incidentally Georg Schnéevoigt's teacher, and Ottokar Novacek.

"The great Joseph Joachim was mainly engaged in playing chamber music during the '80's. I often heard him in the Königliche Hochschule (Royal College). His interpretation of Beethoven's last quartets was an experience that opened up a new world to me. It was the first time that I heard these glorious compositions, which were at that time generally considered quite unplayable. He also gave me much pleasure as a player of sonatas.

" In this connection I must correct the current opinion that in his old age Joachim was a dry pedant who always followed along absolutely straight lines, established once for all. On the contrary, the old man was very impulsive, and he seldom played the same thing twice in the same way."

Sibelius's impressions of the F major quartet opus 59, described in a letter to Wegelius, show how intensely he was absorbed by the Joachim quartet's perfect rendering of Beethoven's compositions and into what strange paths it led his imagination.

" When the adagio was played I thought I was in a colonnade. It was moonlight. On the left was a solid wall, on the other side a beautiful garden with birds of paradise, shells, palms, and so on. All was dead and quiet, the shadows were long and thick, and it smelt like an old library. Nothing was to be heard but sighs. It was Beethoven that sighed. When the theme in F minor was repeated, he sighed an extraordinarily deep sigh. After a time everything changed to large lakes with red water and above them God played the violin."

Faced with this confession today, Sibelius declares that he cannot believe it to have been written by himself; if there had not been ocular evidence, he could have sworn that the letter had been written by someone else. But even if his opinion has changed in the course of time, those lines are worth rescuing from oblivion as evidence of his ability of fantastic absorption and the peculiar, characteristic combination of the sensations of hearing and sight.

While working to improve his technique and absorbing everything of value that the musical life of Berlin could offer him, Sibelius did not give up composing according to his own lights. But external conditions were not calculated to make it easy to concentrate. The noise of the great city, which he experienced for the first time, hampered his inspiration, which drew its sustenance from communing with nature. Life in strange surroundings gave rise to impressions and experiences that upset his spiritual balance at times. The young man, full of the joy of life, experienced times of profound depression in Berlin, of desponding doubt of his ability to fulfill his most cherished purpose. His hard work under Becker's guidance was also of necessity bound to have a paralyzing effect: it consumed the energy that was required for independent composition.

The winter in Berlin was not as productive in quantity as the last few years in Helsingfors had been, but the work he completed, the piano quintet in G minor, represented a victory for Sibelius's individuality, a testimony to his ability to resist the pressure of the outside world. In melodic composition, harmony, and forms based on the foundations laid in Finland, the quintet depicted the anguish and fire of a young mind in episodes that reflected the conflicts during the time in Berlin, but throughout marked by Sibelius's spiritual and musical originality. Indeed, few more convincing proofs can be found of the ability of Sibelius's inspiration to turn inwards, of its imperviousness to ephemeral external impressions and tendencies, than this work of a young man of twenty-four, in which it would be vain to look for impressions of his musical environment.

" It is hard to say," Sibelius himself points out in this connection, " what influences affected me at that time. When I look back at my life, I see that in many respects it has been different from that of other musicians. I think, for instance, of the expression common in German musical literature: ' He had by that time got as far as Schumann (Brahms, Liszt, etc.) . . . .' Such influences that can be pointed at directly, I cannot indicate in my case."

It was with some excitement that young Sibelius awaited the moment when his strict teacher would get to know the G minor quintet, written independently of his actual studies.

The confrontation proved happier than he had dared to hope.

"In spite of his orthodoxy in musical questions, Becker displayed surprising understanding. I put my quintet before him and he studied it with great interest. In the andante movement the old man was really moved. It did not seem at all unpleasant to him to find that the young man had been up to other things besides writing fugues in a strict style."

VIII

TWENTY-FOUR

Norwegian friends — Friends from Finland — An inspired hour — Christmas Eve, 1898 — Musician friends — The first meeting with Robert Kajanus — The Kalevala as a musical subject — Ida Aalberg acts with Joseph Kainz — A visit to Finland — Engaged — Out into the world again.

SIBELIUS's winter in Berlin was outwardly more diffuse, perhaps, than any other period of his training. As a young man of full-blooded temperament, out in the great world on his own for the first time, he found it difficult to shut himself up in his room while life tempted him with so much that was novel as regards both impressions and acquaintances. His open, straightforward nature won him friends easily, in whose company he could pass the time in restaurants and cafés in stimulating conversation about life and art.

" I became acquainted with many interesting people during my studies in Berlin. Among foreigners I saw most of Gabriel Finne, the Norwegian naturalistic author, who was then completing his novel *Doktor Wangs Børn*. Through Finne I got to know many of his countrymen. The society I moved in at that time contained, in general, a very strong Norwegian element and I considered that I was in good company. Thanks to Ibsen and Björnson, Norwegians were very much the vogue in Berlin, and they made no secret of being conscious of their prestige. When a Norwegian came into some small restaurant where Scandinavians used to forgather, he displayed a self-consciousness in his behavior, as if he were permeated by the consciousness: *civis Romanus sum!*

" Of course, literature was much discussed among us. Besides the great Norwegians, Strindberg was the focus of discussion. Georg Brandes, the great Danish critic, was also keenly debated.

" I found it hard," Sibelius confesses, " to share the general rapture for Georg Brandes. He has in general meant very little to me. Outside the group of typically northern authors I was captivated as a young man more by such an author as E. T. A. Hoffmann, the romantic. Nor did Brandes later play the same part for me as he did for many another of my generation. He is too cold and clear, which is very much out of my line. It was only with his book on Goethe that he attracted me more. Much in it appears to me simply inspired, but much impresses me, too, as purely cynical."

A daily companion among his own countrymen was Adolf Paul, who was thus able in Berlin to continue the study of his peculiar friend that he had begun in Helsingfors. The Berlin section of A Book about a Man reveals fresh and more complicated aspects of Sibelius. It describes periods of despondency, of despair; it shows how the young artist grows to manhood in struggling with the problems of existence and his own personality.

In one episode Paul describes how the somber powers within Sibelius sought an outlet in an inspired moment:

" He seated himself at the piano and improvised — softly — dreamily — searchingly. Gradually the wandering ideas united in a definite thought — it took the lead, developed the whole organically; and in a dignified, simple, and feeling manner a melody came forth under his fingers in slow rhythm and faithfully expressed the incomprehensible sensations that swept momentarily through his soul — only to be forgotten immediately.

" It complained in dumb suffering of harsh oppression — it wove itself closer in longing, in powerful, irresistible longing for liberty — rising to conscious captivity's painful cry of terror, to die away again in dumb

85

complaint. And then it returned with memories of times gone by; memories of childhood came tiptoeing in airy pizzicatos with forgotten gay harmonies; gracefully they caressed them in playful coquetry — temptingly they spread them out in shy, undulating arpeggios like shimmering veils in an elfin dance — and then tripped away again, dragging them provokingly and temptingly after them. But they were caught up by the moods that had evoked them. And united in vehement opposition to all that is unnatural, to falsehood and tyrannical power, they piled themselves up into enormous masses of sound — thunderous clouds, from which a flash of hope's thorough conviction burst forth in the theme sustained fortissimo by brilliant, splendid major chords.

" He became more and more inspired — broader and more overwhelming came the harmonies — the masses of sound grew ever mightier. The old piano simply quaked.

" Suddenly he stopped and began to walk up and down the room."

The description gives us a glimpse into the moods of the G minor quintet. We find new accents, a new earnestness, a new depth.

Sibelius celebrated Christmas Eve, 1889, with Werner Söderhjelm and some other countrymen. This select circle had the pleasure of hearing Sibelius celebrate the festival by executing Vieuxtemps's *Ballade et Polonaise!* A unique situation: the composer of *Voces Intimæ* and the fourth symphony devoting himself to interpreting this typical virtuoso piece of the middle of the century!

"I played with all the necessary brilliancy and, of course, scored a great success," says Sibelius jokingly. "By that time, however, I had already given up my dream of becoming a great violinist. I had become resigned and had realized that my real call was in another direction."

A special group was formed by the young musical friends, with whom Sibelius played chamber music.

"I played chamber music as often as I had a chance, and the repertory included my own compositions. My usual fellow-musicians were Theodore Spiering, later a conductor in America, Klingenberg, the pianist, and Fini Henriques, the Danish composer, who remains a close friend of mine to this day. Henriques had in his qualifications and adaptiveness all that I lacked. I thought I discerned something quite uncommon in him, he seemed to me to be a new Mozart."

At any rate Sibelius was modest in his youth!

During the gay meetings of this circle there was once a temporary depression owing to the non-arrival of remittances from home. Sibelius and Henriques discovered a simple method of solving the difficulty. They went to a variety show, introduced themselves to the manager as famous musicians from Finland and Denmark, and offered to give a performance. The occasion came off, the two celebrities performed with great success, received twenty marks (less than five dollars) as their fee and an offer of a fortnight's engagement at a " princely " salary. The offer was tempting, but it was not necessary to accept it, because relief was forthcoming in the shape of financial supplies from home.

In Berlin Sibelius met Robert Kajanus for the first time. I have already indicated the reasons why this acquaintance was not made before: the schism between the orchestra and the musical academy had in its consequences gone to considerable lengths in personal relations. This first meeting of two outstanding figures in the musical life of Finland, who subsequently were closely connected, took place after a concert at which Kajanus introduced his *Aino* symphony to the Berlin audience.

" Acquaintance with this work was of thrilling importance to me. It opened my eyes to the wonderful opportunities the *Kalevala* offered for musical expression. Earlier attempts to interpret the national epos in music had not encouraged imitation. And the environment in which I had grown up was as far removed from the *Kalevala* as possible. My mother and my Swedish grandmother had loved poetry of a very differ-

88

ent kind and had aroused my liking for it. In my youth the *Kalevala* was not the educational equipment of every home in Finland as it became later. Nevertheless, I remember that the Kullervo myth occupied my imagination at school. After hearing Kajanus's *Aino* symphony the thought of creating a work myself with a subject chosen from our national epos began to occupy my fancy more and more.

" At about the time of Kajanus's concert I witnessed the appearance of another countryman, or rather countrywoman, before the critical Berlin public. I saw our celebrated actress Ida Aalberg act with Joseph Kainz in, if I remember rightly, *Romeo and Juliet.* During the first acts her German was irreproachable, but there was a falling off as the play proceeded and in the final scenes she was so carried away that her lines were almost unintelligible. Her wonderful acting saved the situation, however, and the whole thing was a great success. Naturally, I was proud to see a Finnish actress appear with Germany's greatest actor."

While Sibelius was still in Berlin, he received news from home that the first two movements of his piano quintet had been performed with great approval from the critics at a musical evening in the musical academy on May 5, 1890. Shortly after, the young composer started on his way home across the Baltic to prepare for a fresh journey farther south.

During his short stay in Finland, Sibelius frequently visited the Järnefelt family. The liking that had already arisen between him and the youngest daughter of the house now burst into full bloom, and in the autumn of 1890 Jean Sibelius became engaged to Aino Järnefelt. It is scarcely necessary to mention that Jean Sibelius's female relations were delighted to see the unruly genius decide to take such a serious step as marriage. The engagement also gave general satisfaction to the Järnefelt family, to the strict father as much as anyone. General Järnefelt, who had been educated in a different period and to other ideals, strangely enough revealed a profound understanding of the musical originality of his future son-in-law, and he was much attracted by his open, hearty nature; from the first they were on the best of terms, the old aristocrat and the young artist. It contributed a good deal towards their understanding that Sibelius, though brought up in a Swedish home, had been to a Finnish school and had, while young, formed views on patriotic problems that made it possible for him without reserve to enter into the interests and ideas of a truly Finnish house.

The young bridegroom appears quite lifelike in a description given forty years later by his brother-in-law, Arvid Järnefelt, in his charming work *My Parents' Romance:*

" Sibelius was at that time really so full of life, so carried away by the pulsating actuality of life, so full of general enthusiasm, that he was bound to charm everyone who came in contact with him. He was a youth who could enjoy everything, a good cigar, conversation, gay company, the life of nature. When one saw him in the country, even if it were in a meadow, he was able to live his own full life even there: a bird twitters — he pricks up his ears, a shepherdess calls — the melody enters his soul forever. He absorbed everything that each passing hour caused to bloom, all that reached his ear, that his eye beheld. He lived every moment so intensively that at times he really recalled an animal, a fish jumping in a rapid or a young hunting dog that gasps for breath as it scents game — or a bird that, even when sitting still, turns its head in order to hear every rustle and to catch all that living reality has to tell it."

Before Sibelius left Finland he had the satisfaction of hearing his B major quartet, composed in the previous summer, successfully performed at a concert on October 13, 1890.

Then Sibelius started for Vienna.

IX

THE LAST WINTER

OF STUDY

*The struggle between Wagnerians and Brahmsians
— Johannes Brahms, Anton Bruckner, Hans Richter
— Sibelius and Karl Goldmark — The overture in
E major — Sibelius's first Runeberg songs — A ballet
scene for orchestra — First drafts of the Kullervo
symphony.*

N arriving in the beautiful city on the Danube,
Sibelius found himself face to face with a situation to which he had already grown accustomed in Berlin: a struggle to the death between Wagnerians and
Brahmsians. Possibly the struggle was carried on here
with all the more fanaticism on either side, seeing that
the Wagnerians in Vienna had a living idol round
whom to form a guard: the great Anton Bruckner, in
whose broad, heroic style, majestic theme-building and
richly glittering orchestral coloring they found a re-

flection of the art that had enchanted them in the maestro in Bayreuth.

Sibelius had been provided by Busoni with a letter of introduction to Brahms. The letter was in a jesting tone, characteristic both of Busoni personally and of his friendly and frank relationship to Sibelius. " *Seiner nordischen Herkunft gemäss,*" Busoni wrote, " *ist er später entwickelt wie wir* . . . (True to his northern origin, he has developed later than we . . .) ." Whether it was due to this half-jesting expression that was not intended to be misunderstood or to some other circumstance, Busoni's letter of introduction failed completely in its object.

"Brahms stubbornly refused to see me. From a friend, whom I had asked to put in a word for me, I heard that when my ' case ' was reported Brahms put the well-known question of Schubert: ' *Kann er was?* (Can he do anything?) ' — ' Yes, he has written a good quartet.' This distinction must have seemed scarcely sufficient in the case of an otherwise entirely unknown young man from the north, for the maestro did not relent and I only made his personal acquaintance some months after my arrival, by chance at the Café Leidinger. This place was one of the most popular and fashionable meeting-places in the Vienna of that day, and Brahms seemed very strange in such surroundings with his ill-fitting clothes, stained by cigar

ash, and his unkempt, bearded face. Brahms, it is well
known, never took any trouble about his appearance."

Sibelius has no recollection of having had any great
spiritual benefit from his meeting with Brahms. It was
scarcely one of Brahms's failings to take any interest
in youthful talents or confirm their faith by words of
paternal encouragement.

" Anton Bruckner I never met personally. But I was
present at the original performance of his sextet. I was
sitting quite close to him and had a good opportunity
of observing him. A kindly little old man, who seemed
rather lost in the world. He was short of stature, but
disproportionately stout. The joking Viennese called
him ' ein Rhinozeros mit Nachtigallenkehle (a rhi-
noceros with the throat of a nightingale) . ' "

A very different reception from that of Brahms
awaited Sibelius at Hans Richter's, the celebrated
Wagner conductor, whose advice he sought at Martin
Wegelius's suggestion.

" As leader of the orchestra at the Court Opera, Hans
Richter was a powerful man in the musical world of
Vienna. He received me in a very friendly way and listened attentively to what I had to say, in spite of my
having called on him during a rehearsal of Tristan and
Isolde. What I most wanted at that stage of my development was guidance in instrumentation. Richter was
a convinced Wagnerian, but not a fanatic, seeing that

he recommended a teacher for me from the opposite camp.

" It was on Richter's advice that I studied with Robert Fuchs, a trained orchestrator and prolific composer in the sphere of both ecclesiastical and secular music, but best known for his orchestral serenades and therefore called ' Serenaden-Fuchs ' in private.

" Fuchs was one of the leaders of the Brahmsians, but externally as unlike his lord and master as possible. A handsome old gentleman, slender, well groomed, with old-fashioned graceful manners — altogether a distinguished personality."

In his efforts to secure a varied training in the technique of orchestration Sibelius came in contact with the third celebrity among living Viennese composers: Karl Goldmark, who was then living in the glory of a reputation that was almost comparable to that of Brahms and Bruckner, though founded on another basis.

" I had a letter of introduction from Martin Wegelius to Goldmark. It was not easy to gain access to the famous man, who used from time to time to cut himself off from all connection with the outer world in order to work undisturbed. On November 12 he granted me an audience at last and it passed much more happily than might have been expected. When I asked Goldmark if he was willing to instruct me in instrumentation, he replied: ' *Ja, ich rathe sehr gern einem jungen Künstler* (Yes, I am very ready to advise a young artist) .' It was the first time in my life that I had heard myself called ' *junger Künstler*,' and of course I was frightfully proud.

" I knew that Goldmark had not accepted pupils for several years and the fact that he made an exception in my case was a favor to be appreciated. It was agreed that I should return to him as soon as I had completed a composition, when he would look through it and make any necessary alterations."

Goldmark was entirely occupied at that time by his own work of composition. He was a composer of whom the general public wanted its fill, he was overwhelmed with orders and commissions, and the fees he obtained were among the highest that could be secured by any composer at that time. Goldmark had very little spare time for teaching, and this explains why the instruction he gave Sibelius was mostly of a consultative character. He gave his lessons at long intervals and confined himself as a rule to summary opinions from which his pupil had to extract what wisdom he could. Goldmark's teaching, therefore, did not provide Sibelius with what he had expected; for methodical training in the art of instrumentation he had to resort to the conscientious, patient Fuchs. However, the personal relations between master and pupil remained excellent to the end.

" Goldmark had the reputation of being a very haughty, conventional man. He was never so to me, and I, too, was very frank with him. My first attempt as an orchestral composer, an overture, he pulled to pieces completely. I then wrote another overture that found greater favor in his eyes. This work, Overture in E major, was performed that spring at an orchestral concert in Helsingfors.

" Goldmark's criticism, by the way, was quite justified. My orchestral style was then still governed entirely by my chamber-music style, from which I found it very difficult to get away — very naturally, as all my former instrumental compositions had been in that direction. It was only when I was back in Finland, later in the '90's, that I developed a real orchestral style.

" Neither my studies with Fuchs nor those with Goldmark were of much importance for my inner development. In all I did I was a ' strange bird.' In the midst of my work of studying to become a trained orchestrator I could not resist paying homage once more to the great love of my youth: chamber music. I wrote a piano quartet in C major, with the composition of which my teachers had nothing to do. I also wrote many songs independently, including three that later

97

formed part of my first cycle of songs, *Seven Songs by Runeberg.*"

It is not necessary to mention more than this one circumstance — Runeberg's poetry as a source of inspiration for Sibelius in Vienna — to find further confirmation of the thesis regarding Sibelius's complete independence of his temporary environment. If we want to find a tribute to specific Viennese impressions in his work of that time we can point out the brilliantly orchestrated *A Ballet Scene*, performed for the first time in Helsingfors at the same concert as the E major overture. This apparent concession to environment was, however, outweighed many times over by the proof of loyalty to his own inner development that is evident in the fact that it was during the winter in Vienna that the first drafts of the *Kalevala* myth *Kullervo* were made.

" Another of my most characteristic works in the early '90's," Sibelius points out, " was conceived in Vienna, for I began an octet for strings, flute, and clarinet, the motif of which later provided the thematic material for *En Saga.*

" I generally worked strictly at my development in Vienna. The winter of 1890–1 was considerably more productive than the previous winter in Berlin. I was able to concentrate to a greater degree than before. I already perceived more clearly the objects I had to aim at. I was surer of myself and did not let myself be led astray in my idea of my vocation in spite of the comparatively small understanding that my teachers showed of the special style that I now began to realize was my strong point."

X

ARTISTS' LIFE IN

VIENNA

*Old Vienna — The power of musical traditions —
Johann Strauss — Life among musicians — Member
of an anti-Wagner orchestra — A curious order —
Pauline Lucca's receptions — Pauline Lucca and
Adelina Patti.*

𝕎HILE Sibelius the composer, guided by unfailing instinct, followed the dictates of his inner being, the young man moved with an open mind in the gay Imperial city on the Danube.

" At last I have come to a place that was made for me! " Sibelius exclaims joyfully in his first letter from Vienna to Martin Wegelius, dated October 25, 1890. Fresh surroundings, more richly colored than the German capital, a lighter atmosphere, livelier people. Sibelius got on simply splendidly in Vienna.

" Vienna was at that time quite the old Vienna.

Johann Strauss, junior, was still living and now and then one had a chance of seeing him conduct his waltzes. He was sixty-five, but led his orchestra with the fire of a young man. Since that time I have had a liking for Strauss waltzes that has lasted throughout my life.

"Vienna lived entirely in music. The power of the musical traditions was great. The air was full of memories, not only of Schubert's and Beethoven's days, but also of Mozart's time. Among the oral traditions about Mozart I remember it being said that he could never get the overture to *The Marriage of Figaro* played fast enough: it should have been played *prestissimo*.

"I lived in the part of the town called Alte Wieden in a house at the corner of Karlsgasse and Waaggasse, next to the house in which Gluck had once dwelt. It was only a few steps from my quarters to the Landesstrasse, from which one could see Schönbrunn, the favorite palace of the Emperor Francis Joseph. You could often see lights in the windows of the palace at five or six in the morning: the old Emperor was an early riser.

"One of the most powerful impressions during the early part of my stay in Vienna was when I heard the *Rakoczy March* for the first time. Early one morning I was on my way to Goldmark's house in the Alser-

101

strasse. The day was foggy, the air was cold and damp. Suddenly through the fog I heard the tramp of approaching cavalry and all at once the band struck up the exciting march. I was red in the face from excitement when I got to Goldmark's."

Sibelius lived intensely in Vienna. The future took on a brighter hue than before. Growing consciousness of his creative gifts inclined him to look upon the small annoyances of life from an exalted philosophical point of view. The demons of melancholy and depression still burdened his soul at times, but more rarely than in Berlin. All was overshadowed by the joyful certainty that he was on the right road, that he would soon acquire the knowledge that was necessary to convert the visions he had caught in the far-sightedness of his inspiration into living works of art.

Full of inexhaustible vitality, Sibelius divided his time between hard work in developing himself and excursions into the rich and beautiful world around him.

Sibelius found faithful companions in the crowd of young musicians and artists who formed his daily society. Through these friends Sibelius joined an anti-Wagner orchestra of students, to whose accompaniment he once played the first movement of Mendelssohn's violin concerto. This was, as far as we know, the last time that Sibelius carried away an audito-

SIBELIUS IN VIENNA, 1891

rium on a festive occasion by his skill as a violin soloist.

" I must have been surrounded by some kind of halo among my intimates, for owing to it I received a commission that was and remained unique in my experience. A circus manager unexpectedly required a new march for his band and one of my friends described me to the worried man in beguiling terms as the man made for the job. The matter was extremely urgent and I composed the march in the course of the afternoon. I hope it proved successful."

Another world opened up to Sibelius in the salon of Pauline Lucca, the famous singer. At her far-famed receptions one met not only the leaders of art and music, but also a great many celebrities, attracted by the opportunity of seeing many illustrious artists at close quarters. An aristocratic assembly ennobled by art.

Martin Wegelius, untiringly active in the interests of his gifted pupil in distant Vienna, had written a letter to Pauline Lucca recommending him very warmly to the illustrious lady. In January 1891 Sibelius had the distinction of being invited for the first time to a musical evening at Lucca's. This attention was followed by several fresh invitations in the course of time.

" There was a festive brilliance at Lucca's recep-

tions. A select company, a high-class program. There
was much good music, but also much dancing.

"Lucca herself often sang at her receptions — always ' for the last time.' In spite of her age — she had
recently celebrated her fiftieth birthday — she sang
adorably. She sang the ' Habanera ' from *Carmen* incomparably. Lucca's singing seemed to me infinitely
more full of feeling than Adelina Patti's, who gave a
concert about the same time in Vienna, for which I
succeeded in securing standing-room at a mad price.
However, I still remember Patti's rendering of the
Il Bacio valse: her voice sounded exactly like a clarinet."

Sibelius was a young man from a small country, as
yet unknown to the world, but possessing a natural self-
esteem that did not allow him to try to become familiar
with the leaders of art and society by ingratiating manners. He has, therefore, no profound personal impressions of the celebrities he saw at close quarters at
Pauline Lucca's. The fascinating gifts — wealth of imagination, humor, a lively intellect, a playful disposition, warmth of feeling and mind — that might easily
have brought the youthful stranger into fruitful contact
with many remarkable personalities, whose acquaintance would have been of value to him in more than
one respect, these gifts Sibelius preferred to employ
for spreading joy in the intimate circle of his contemporaries. The young man already adopted the attitude

that became characteristic of the celebrated composer in the course of time, always preferring to choose people in his life according to the exchange of ideas, not the benefits, they could offer him.

We must certainly not imagine young Sibelius as a courtier in Lucca's salon. On those occasions, probably very rare, on which he tried to divest himself of his formal stiffness and behave with the ease of a man of the world, the result, if we are to believe his own account, was not invariably quite successful.

"Once I was guilty of a grave offense. Among Lucca's guests was a Princess of Reuss, a lady of extremely high rank; if I am not mistaken, a cousin of the Emperor Wilhelm. In my anxiety to be polite I committed the crime against etiquette of offering her a chair, although I had not yet been presented — a frightful mistake for which I was taken to task in a friendly way by Filip Forstén, my only fellow-countryman in the brilliant assembly, who hurried forward very much upset."

We must allow this amusing episode in the experiences of a young northerner in the vernal city of the Habsburgs to close our description of Sibelius's studies in Vienna — a period of work and pleasant dreams of the future which he himself recalls with regret.

His years of study had come to an end. He was on the threshold of manhood.

XI

HOME AGAIN

*Inspiring surroundings — The Päivälehti circle —
Karl August Tavaststjerna — Axel Gallén — The ad-
vent of Kullervo — The concert on April 28, 1892
— Marriage — A honeymoon in Karelia — Poet
friends in Kuopio — Minna Canth — Intensive work.*

ON returning from Vienna early in the summer of
1891, Sibelius joined his mother, sister, and
brother in Lovisa. Full of ideas and impelled by a burning desire to compose, he remained throughout the autumn and the greater part of the winter in the town
of bright memories of his childhood in order to concentrate on completing the works he had begun in
Vienna. His sojourn in Lovisa was, however, interrupted by trips to the capital, which he visited in order
that the society of his friends should provide the intellectual stimulus the country town was not able to
give him.

Finland was undergoing a period of intense spiritual

activity. The Russian attack launched in the late winter of 1890 against Finnish laws and rights had evoked
patriotic enthusiasm that surged across the country
as inspiringly, intoxicatingly, and regeneratingly as a
storm in spring. The imperative watchword of the
time was, by means of increased activity in all spheres
of life, to strengthen national confidence and powers
of resistance.

Through his future brothers-in-law, the young Järne-
felts, Sibelius was initiated into one of the hotbeds of
this patriotic revival. At the time of the first Russian
attacks young Finland had established a newspaper,
Päivälehti, with the object of proclaiming the thoughts
and ideals of a new generation in the burning literary,
general cultural, and political questions of the day.
The leading personalities on the paper were Juhani
Aho, Arvid Järnefelt, and Eero Erkko, and round this
triumvirate a crowd of young authors and artists
grouped themselves. Painting was numerously and
worthily represented in this coterie by Eero Järnefelt,
Axel Gallén, Pekka Halonen, and the Swede, Louis
Sparre, who entered completely into the feelings of
his Finnish friends.

Sibelius was one of the representatives of music in
this circle of authors and artists. In spite of the dis-
similarity in professional interests and training, he was
bound by strong ties to the enthusiasts, who went in

for other forms of spiritual athletics. Like himself, the majority of them were animated by the wealth of ideas and zeal for work that usually follows the first journeys abroad; like himself they had made up their minds to draw inspiration for their art from the source of Finnish nationalistic enthusiasm.

The same patriotic spirit, though based on a different foundation from the Finnish nationalistic one, was found by Sibelius in the group in which the great painter Albert Edelfelt's bright, noble personality, uniting, conciliating, brought clarity and breadth to the discussions and a spirit of effective, energetic optimism. Sibelius also found great spiritual encouragement among the standard-bearers of the young Finnish-Swedish literature, in Tavaststjerna, Lybeck, and Procopé. The incarnation, in his whole personality, of chivalrous tolerance and raised far above all narrow-minded fanaticism, the young composer met with as ready sympathy for his art and his style among these Swedish friends as among those to whom he was drawn by community of language and cultural and political views.

The case of Sibelius was not an isolated one. Both Gallén and Aho had intimate personal friends among Swedes, and Tavaststjerna was at this time seeking for connections beyond the language frontier in his vexed reaction against what he called " guild-Swedomania."

The idealist enthusiasm, the feeling that in reality all were fighting for the same cause, was in general so strong among young Finnish and Swedish artists and men of culture in the idyllic Finland of the '90's that it victoriously burst the barriers of language and party. The threat of danger from the east welded them together. The contrasts between them acted beneficently, inciting them to competition without jealousy, not in a crippling, sterilizing way.

The artistic friendship that united Axel Gallén and Karl August Tavaststjerna at this time was symbolical of the relationship between Finns and Swedes. They had both taken up their abode in Malm, where the newly-wed Tavaststjerna lived in the white building next to the railway station, still extant at the present day and easily discernible to passing travelers from the train.

During his trips to Helsingfors, Sibelius established close contact with both Tavaststjerna and Gallén. He often visited his friend Tavaststjerna in his seclusion in the country. Tavaststjerna's personality, on which life had left its traces, made a deep impression on him. He relates the following:

" Tavaststjerna was engaged in dramatizing *Hårda Tider* (*Hard Times*) and very worried by the thought as to how the work, not yet published as a novel, would be received by the critics. He was already very embittered, experienced periods of the deepest despondency in struggling with the difficulties he encountered as much as any of a financial nature. But he restrained himself in the presence of strangers. He endeavored to treat his guests with the greatest friendliness and consideration in matters both great and small, revealing his extremely sensitive nature in all things. There was something strangely pathetic about him. You seldom meet a nobler character.

" It was a great day when he visited us in the following winter in our first home in Helsingfors. A copy of his *Poems* lay expectantly on the table. The volume was much thumbed; it bore clear traces of having been read assiduously. Tavaststjerna noticed this. He was much moved and looked at me almost embarrassed, with tears in his eyes. All he said was: ' This is the best criticism I could have had.'

" Axel Gallén was of different fiber, harder and tougher. He was a few years younger than Tavaststjerna and looked into the future more brightly than he. As yet unbroken by the trials and disappointments of an artist's life, he was full of optimism, vigor, and creative force. He was talkative and lively, and frequently enlivened our meetings with wonderful tales of his travels as a student. He had seen a good deal of the world and was able to benefit by his experiences, both grave and gay. I fancy his society was very good for Tavaststjerna during the latter's dark hours.

" With Tavaststjerna's untimely death I lost a friend who could have taught me much. With Gallén I was in close contact during the whole of the '90's and we were on the best of terms even after our paths had separated. We continued thus until Gallén's death. We did not meet very often, but each meeting was a great day for both of us. Gallén and I were very good friends. He was a fiery soul.

" When a book was published a few years ago in honor of Gallén's memory, I was asked to contribute the papers I had received from him. I searched among my papers and, among other things, discovered these lines, which excellently indicate the terms on which Gallén and I were. They were written in reply to my congratulations on the occasion of his fiftieth birthday:

Linudden

May 3, 1915

Dear Sibelius:

You will forgive my using the typewriter, for, if anyone, you should know that my hand is tired. On my fiftieth birthday you wrote me an introduction to the palace of the immortals, a royal charter of nobility, that requires no countersigning, thanks to which I could leave my couch of laurels unmade for posterity, but you know how pretentious one is at our age: that one would rather destroy oneself in the orgies with which our labors tempt us, independently of any other verdict than that of our artistic conscience. Our muse, for, no doubt, we have one, is as impatient of homage as the white mare in a triumphal procession tires of prancing under the bridle and longs for the pastures of the meadow.

You, Sibelius, were my equal and a close companion in the days when we staked out our paths and have since then been an admired example to me. Both of us have so much to do that we have no time to " associate," but it often seems to me that we meet in the spirit.

At the dinner on April 26, at which I had in vain looked forward to having you and your wife as my partners at table, I was able to stand my ground against the storm of homage by thinking of Cervantes's splendid hero, who, too, was not scared. . . . The dear people did all they could to spoil my shy disposition.

Soon it will be your turn and then: Evoe, Evoe! You will not need, however, to compare yourself to the Knight of La Mancha, for you have never had to defend yourself against windmills and hogsheads. Your letter was so beautiful that I had to wrap my profound feeling and gratitude in this garb in order to hide my emotion.

Yours,

Gallén

Both Tavaststjerna and Gallén exerted an influence on Sibelius: Tavaststjerna as the author of the poems that gave birth to some of the most enchanting productions of Sibelius's lyrical inspiration; Gallén by his strong fantastic absorption in Finland's mythical antiquity, in many points related to that of Sibelius, in many unlike it.

Surrounded by powerful creative talents and seething activity on all hands, Sibelius himself worked with burning zeal at his own great, newly forming contribution. He set the Kullervo myth to music, having, as already mentioned, made the first drafts of it in Vienna. For once his outer environment was in harmony with his work. The glowing patriotic enthusiasm around him; the society of the Järnefelt family, with its pronounced Finnish national interests; the confidential exchange of thoughts with Gallén, who was at that time engaged in completing his great *Kalevala* triptych; finally, Sibelius's own desire, free from all fetters, to convert the knowledge he had acquired during years of doubt and searching into a work filled to the brim by his personality — all this combined towards the proud creation that became the revolutionary prologue to his deed of manhood: *Kullervo*, a symphonic poem in five movements for large orchestra, soloists, and choir, a thoroughly revolutionary work, in which a lavishly rich romantic imagination, combined with intense love of nature and vivid naturalism in technique and use of forms, conjured forth a somberly beautiful prehistoric world, embracing the mysticism of the wilds, colorful idylls, and scenes of defiant heroism and moving tragedy in predestined unity.

Kullervo was performed for the first time on April 28, 1892, with the composer as conductor. The work was received with such enthusiasm as had never yet been accorded a Finnish composition. The large audience surrendered unconditionally. Its enthusiasm was not due to its fully understanding the revolutionary com-position — that would have been expecting almost too much. But the voice of genius spoke so mightily, so overpoweringly, throughout the whole work from the first bar to the last, that there was nothing for the dumb-founded hearers to do but to rejoice and admire, even in the parts they were unable to understand.

The critics followed the example of the audience. In reading their critiques today one is half tempted to smile at the touching efforts of the critical experts to show that they fully appreciated the means and de-signs in the novel and great art that confronted them with the suddenness of revelation. None dared run the risk of appearing uncomprehending. In short, the critics distinguished themselves.

Sibelius had succeeded irresistibly. With Kullervo the composer had, at the age of twenty-six, won for himself a position among Finnish artists that none could dispute. He need no longer doubt his genius.

114

MRS. AINO SIBELIUS

With a clear conscience he could plan his life on the calling of an artist, defying material difficulties in the calm consciousness that the great compensation in the form of the attainment of the highest artistic values was assured him. On June 10, 1892 Jean Sibelius and Aino Järnefelt were married. The honeymoon was spent in Karelia, in the neighborhood of the village of Lieksa on the eastern shore of Lake Pielisjärvi.

In this Sibelius satisfied the longing for the wilds, born of national romanticism, that had at that time taken hold of so many of his friends. Gallén had at the same time gone to Kuusamo, Louis Sparre and Emil Wikström had decided to travel to Kuhmoniemi and Russian Karelia, and Eero Järnefelt and Juhani Aho were to start on a long journey at the end of the summer from Kuopio over Koli, Pielisjärvi and Pan-kakoski to Tuulijärvi across the border.

" As a musician and as the composer of *Kullervo*," Sibelius points out, " I was particularly anxious to visit the Karelian countryside, for there I had an opportunity of hearing runes sung after having become so intensely engrossed in the world whose moods, fate, and people they describe. The language of sound that I had employed in *Kullervo* was considered to give such thorough and true expression of Finnish scenery and the soul of the Finnish people that many were unable

115

to explain it in any other way than that I had made direct use of folk-melodies, especially of the accents of runic song, in my work. The genuinely Finnish tone of *Kullervo* could, however, not have been achieved in this way, for the simple reason that at the time the work was composed I was not acquainted with my supposed model. First I composed *Kullervo*; then I went to Karelia to hear, for the first time in my life, the *Kalevala* runes from the lips of the people. This may seem strange, but it was actually the case."

Here we find a convincing refutation of the opinion, maintained with peculiar stubbornness, especially abroad, that the specifically Finnish coloring in Sibelius's early art is due to his basing his compositions on the direct appropriation of Finnish folk-melodies.

In Pielisjärvi Sibelius composed three songs to words by Runeberg: " Under Strandens Granar (Under the Firs on the Shore)," " Kyssens Hopp (The Hope of the Kiss)," and " Till Frigga (To Frigga)." With the three songs he had composed in Vienna and " Jägargossen (The Young Sportsman)," written in the summer of 1891 during a visit to Martin Wegelius's country house, Vikan, in Pojo, he completed a series which he published in the autumn of 1892 as his first opus published by itself: " *Seven Songs by Runeberg*, composed by Jean Sibelius. Helsingfors: The Otava Publishing Company, 1892."

After spending a few weeks at Pielisjärvi the young couple settled in the neighborhood of Kuopio. In Kuopio Sibelius saw his friend Tavaststjerna again and Juhani Aho, who was about to start on his journey to Russian Karelia. Tavaststjerna and his wife had taken up their abode in the flourishing midland town of Kuopio in order to assist Aho in translating into Finnish *Uramo Croft*, the dramatized version of *Hard Times* that Tavaststjerna was finishing. The two poets saw a great deal of Minna Canth, the greatest celebrity of the capital of Savolax, who was herself engaged on her social-revolutionary drama *Sylvi*. Sibelius's young wife had been acquainted with the famous lady at the time General Järnefelt was Governor of Kuopio. The connection was therefore natural. Sibelius has a clear recollection of her:

" Minna Canth was a cheerful woman, full of ideas and keen interest in the phenomena of life in the most varied spheres. She was very stout and therefore avoided physical exercise. But her mind was all the more alert. She radiated constant energy and vitality, enthroned on her sofa at the coffee table.

" Minna Canth was very well disposed towards me as to other progressive artists. I was invited to her house a couple of times with Tavaststjerna. The conversation was very lively, and when subjects of conversation failed, our hostess had another item ready for her program. Minna Canth was at that time keenly interested in spiritualistic experiments, and one of the amusements to which she was fond of treating her guests was table-turning. I was present on a couple of these occasions. The others watched, whether with feigned or real interest I do not know. But I was very much of a doubting Thomas and was unable to hide it entirely. I noticed that my skepticism did not please Minna Canth at all."

In this way the summer of 1892 passed — in work and in the stimulating exchange of thoughts in the shelter of the idyllic capital of Savolax.

XII

PRODUCTIVE YEARS

Teacher at the musical academy and orchestral school
— A legend — An opera that never saw the light —
Karelian music — Vårsång (Spring Song) — Off to
Italy — A visit to Bayreuth.

WHEN autumn set in, Sibelius moved to Helsingfors to take up the post of teacher of theory at
the musical academy and second violin in the string
quartet of the academy. At the same time he occupied
the post of teacher of theory in the orchestral school
of the Philharmonic Society — a post that Robert Kajanus, a sworn supporter of Sibelius's art since the
Kullervo concert, had established solely in order to improve his financial position.

" This was not the only result of Kajanus's energetic
interest in me as a progressive young composer. It was
of immense importance to me that he placed his orchestra so completely at the service of my art, partly
by himself industriously performing my works, partly

by placing the orchestra at my disposal whenever I cared to try the effects of combinations of sounds and generally to see how my new scores sounded in reality. Kajanus's encouraging attitude furthered my development as an orchestral composer during the 1890's in a great measure and was of value to me, too, in other respects at a time when our musical life was led more or less by amateurs. I owe Kajanus a debt of great gratitude for what he did for me, not only in my youth, but also at a later period, when the really understanding champions of my art were not too numerous."

Sibelius's duties as a teacher were certainly no sinecure.

" When they were hardest," Sibelius recalls, " I had occasionally as many as thirty hours' teaching in a week. Obviously, this affected my composing, though, perhaps, not so much as one was inclined to think afterwards. I was young then and thought I had time and strength enough for everything."

In addition to teaching, Sibelius worked at the completion of the works he had begun during the summer, songs and short pieces for the piano, but above all an orchestral work of appreciable size.

This had an interesting history:

" After the success of *Kullervo*," says Sibelius, " Robert Kajanus once pointed out to me how desirable it was to have a piece by me in the regular repertory of the orchestra written for the general public and not making too great demands on their powers of concentration and comprehension. This would be an advantage both for the orchestra and for my popularity as a composer, Kajanus said. I was not at all disinclined to write a piece in a more popular style. When I got to work I found that some notes I had made in Vienna were very suitable for adaptation. In this way *En Saga* appeared."

En Saga was, perhaps, not quite what Kajanus had expected — not the easily understood *da capo* piece that an enthusiastic audience would want to hear time after time. But instead it became a brilliant orchestral poem, a romantic tale of chivalry in the glittering colors of realistic instrumentation which, when skillfully interpreted both in Finland and abroad, proved an appreciated item in any serious symphonic program, especially after the composer had revised the work at the end of the century.

In the summer of 1893 we again find Sibelius in Kuopio. The author J. H. Erkko was living in the town at the same time, and in conversation with him Sibelius was inspired once more to undertake a *Kalevala* subject, this time in the form of an opera entitled *Veneen Luominen (The Creation of the Boat)*.

" It was originally intended that Erkko should write the book of the opera, but somehow or other I did so myself, while Erkko helped me as literary adviser. During the summer I completed the prologue to the opera and the book. When I returned to Helsingfors in the autumn, I called on Kaarlo Bergbom, the creator of the Finnish operatic stage, to ask for his opinion of the book. He said that it was effective, but too lyrical. In this he was, indeed, right; I realized this at once.

" This sealed the doom of the opera. But the labor I had devoted to carrying out the idea was not entirely wasted, for my fresh absorption in the world of the *Kalevala* gave me the idea for the *Lemminkäinen* suite. In the prologue to the opera I really had one movement of the suite ready made: ' The Swan of Tuonela.' "

Before Sibelius could bring his second *Kalevala* hero into being, he was confronted with other tasks. The Viborg student corporation had approached him with a request that he should write the music for a series of historical tableaux that were to be performed at a soirée arranged by the corporation on November 13, 1893, in aid of national education in eastern Finland. The subjects were taken from the history of Karelia, and many famous historical figures appeared in the tableaux, such as Swedish conquerors and knights and the Tsar Peter.

Sibelius felt very much attracted by the task. Hitherto myths had inspired his creative vein, but his imagination was captivated with equal force by the feelings and moods surrounding the destinies and figures of historical fact. The accompaniment to the historical tableaux, intended and conceived as incidental music, turned under his hand into a series of works of art which, when freed from their original connection, were to come into their own as independent musical compositions, at first in the form of a suite of eight movements, later in a stricter selection in the *Karelia* suite with its Overture, Intermezzo, Ballad, and Alla marcia.

" The Karelia music," Sibelius relates, " was composed during the latter part of the summer of 1893, which I spent at Ruovesi. In this inspiring region I also composed the piano sonata in F major."

The winter of 1893–4 proved very productive. Songs and piano pieces appeared in large numbers. In the spring the beautiful hymn to northern nature was composed, known to us under the name of Vårsång (*Spring Song*), but the atmosphere of which is, perhaps, more correctly rendered by the French title, *La Tristesse du printemps*. At the same time Sibelius wrote a cantata for the university in 1894 to the words of Kasimir Leino, one of his friends in the *Päivälehti* coterie.

Spring Song received its baptism of fire at the eighth public song and musical festival of the Society for

National Education in Vasa. It was performed at the festival concert on June 21, 1894, under the leadership of the composer, with a very peculiar provisional title: " Improvisation for Orchestra." On the same occasion Armas Järnefelt's symphonic poem *Korsholm* was performed for the first time, also under the composer's leadership.

When the labors of the musical festival were over, Sibelius sought to refresh his inspiration by a journey abroad. The young composer's first destination was Italy, where he spent several sunny weeks in visiting Rome, Venice, and other towns.

" It was the first time I had been to Italy," says Sibelius, " and I was equally enchanted by the scenery, the inspiring historical associations, and the people. I have repeated the visit many times since. In fact, whenever I have had the chance I have returned to that lovely country."

From the sunny south Sibelius steered his course to Bayreuth, where he had agreed to meet Armas Järnefelt. The latter was an enthusiastic Wagnerian and was determined at all costs that his brother-in-law, whose lukewarmness towards Wagner hurt him, should hear the master's works in their own surroundings.

The event was a disappointment to Sibelius, or, rather, he was not infected with enthusiasm any more than before. On the contrary, it would seem that the local environment and atmosphere only confirmed him in his aloofness. Sibelius expresses this briefly: "I heard *Tannhäuser* and *Lohengrin* performed superbly, but was not able to feel any fervor for Wagner's art and would not be persuaded to stay and hear the other operas.

"Everything in Bayreuth was adapted for a reverence that seemed forced. If you got into a cab you caught sight of a sign fastened to the back of the driver's seat: 'Historical!' This meant that Wagner had once sat in the cab. The faithful Wagnerians absorbed their master's works in a mood that appeared to have very little in common with real living musical enthusiasm: it was as if they were receiving the Holy Communion.

"I enjoyed my walks in the neighborhood of Bayreuth more than the performances in the Festspielhaus. The scenery round Bayreuth provided views that were among the most poetic one could imagine.

"From Bayreuth I went on to Munich, where I stayed about a month and worked at my *Lemminkäinen* suite. Then I traveled home to take up my work again at the musical academy."

This period coincides with the series of evenings of productive talks with fellow-thinkers round a glass of wine, the memory of which Gallén has recorded in the famous painting that was originally called *Problem*, but appears to posterity as a symbol of the Bohemian artistic life of the '90's, removed from sordid material cares, under the more familiar name of *Symposium*.

The meetings took place in the small popular restaurant of that day.

The regular Symposium circle consisted of Sibelius, Gallén, and Kajanus. Kindred-souled artists took part in the sittings, including Armas Järnefelt, when engagements in Finland and abroad allowed him to be present at the meetings of the circle. Entrance to the circle of the elect was often also permitted to representatives of the profane multitude, if they were thought worthy.

" There was ideal harmony among the leaders," one of these privileged persons testifies. " Each of them contributed in his own way to keep up their good spirits, Gallén with lively sallies, Kajanus with eloquent speeches, frequently of a philosophical nature. Sibelius excelled in lively conversation, alternating between playful jest and gravest earnest. When words failed him, he seated himself at the piano and poured out his soul in endless improvisations, to which those present listened with breathless excitement. Hour after hour passed in this way and no one noticed the flight of time."

" Our sittings," says Sibelius, " were not based on

the treasures of Bacchus to the extent that some may suppose. We allowed our imagination to soar, our thoughts to play. The waves rolled very high. Life passed in review. We discussed the most varied subjects, but always in an optimistic and revolutionary spirit. The way was to be cleared for new ideas in all spheres.

" The Symposium evenings were a great resource to me at a time when I should otherwise have stood more or less alone. The opportunity of exchanging ideas with kindred souls, animated by the same spirit and the same objects, exerted an extremely stimulating influence on me, confirmed me in my purposes, gave me confidence."

Helsingfors was a small town in the '90's, but its society was cultured and an example to many a larger town in its appreciation of art and artists. The maintenance of a high cultural level was, indeed, considered the country's surest defense against the threat from the east, and people realized what they owed to the standard-bearers of culture. The symposia of the geniuses were well known and evoked good-natured, amused commentaries. Legends flourished about them; fantastic rumors circulated about the physical endurance of their members.

But to depict the meetings in a painting, exhibited to the public gaze, was apparently more than good old

Helsingfors could swallow. When Gallén exhibited his painting *Problem* in the autumn of 1894, society was scandalized. Gallén referred to the effect in bitter terms:

" I painted portraits and drew series of pictures and gained the approval of the general and educated public until one day I ventured to exhibit the innermost soul of the brave talker — that is, my own naked ego. My painting *Problem* was the bomb that exploded, and all the splinters hit myself " (Gallén: *Kallela Memoirs*, pp. 51–2).

" The Symposium period," Sibelius goes on, " lasted from the autumn of 1892 to 1895. Then Gallén went abroad and I had to go my own way. The spirit of the '90's never returned.

" At the end of the period, however, I was still imprisoned in the same realm of feeling that had, on the whole, swayed me since I returned from my journeys abroad. My imagination still moved in the realm of the *Kalevala*. I worked at the *Lemminkäinen* cycle that had occupied me since the summer of 1893 and had been brought a good bit nearer completion after my visit to Bayreuth during my stay in Munich. I worked on slowly while I performed my duties at the musical academy. *Lemminkäinen* was my great task, though it did not prevent my finishing other compositions. In the autumn of 1894 I composed a musical recitation for piano, two trumpets, and string orchestra to Rydberg's poem *Skogsrået* (*The Woodnymph*). Soon I found, however, that the material called for more extensive treatment and enlarged the musical recitation to a symphonic poem, which I performed for the first time at a concert of my own compositions in April 1895."

XIII

COMPOSER AND

TEACHER

Sibelius's second Kalevala hero takes shape — The Maid in the Tower, Sibelius's only opera — The Coronation Cantata in 1896 — Sibelius is able to restrict his teaching — Pupils' opinions of Sibelius as a teacher.

URING 1894 and 1895 a great many piano pieces and a number of solo songs to words by Runeberg and Tavaststjerna — for instance, among them the very beautiful *Fågellek (Enticement)* — flowed from the pen of the industrious composer. At this time Finnish poetry enters into Sibelius's work in some songs for male choruses to words from the *Kanteletar* and by Kivi. *Rakastava (The Lover)*, to words from the *Kanteletar*, was later used as a foundation for the well-known suite for string orchestra. *Sydämeni Laulu (The Song of My Heart)*, to words by Kivi, is an affecting expression of a great sorrow Sibelius and his wife suffered.

At the turn of the year 1895–6 the *Lemminkäinen* cycle was at last completed. It consisted of four tone poems: " Lemminkäinen and the Maidens," " Lemminkäinen in Tuonela," " The Swan of Tuonela," " The Return of Lemminkäinen." Sibelius performed them for the first time at a concert of his own compositions in April 1896, and then revised them, presenting the new version at another concert at the beginning of 1897. " The Swan of Tuonela " and " The Return of Lemminkäinen " were revised once more in 1900, when they appeared in their final form.

The autumn of 1896 witnessed the appearance of a work that should almost be considered a curiosity among Sibelius's compositions: his only opera, *The Maid in the Tower*, in one act, to words by Rafael Herzberg, and performed at an evening entertainment on November 7. This piece was purely an incidental composition and the composer himself does not seem inclined to attach any importance to it.

In connection with the coronation of Nicholas II, Sibelius composed a coronation cantata, to words written by Paavo Cajander, which was performed in the courtyard of the university in honor of its Chancellor. It was a tradition that the heir to the Russian throne was the Chancellor of the university.

This occasion was a somber memory for Sibelius. "It was all," he says, "very tragic. The trumpet-blower arrived very drunk and could not be sobered in any way. He started to improvise in the middle of a fugued movement and spoilt the whole impression completely."

On the occasion of university degrees being conferred in 1897 Sibelius, who was at the time deputizing as teacher of music at the university, composed a cantata to words by A. W. Forsman.

The summer of 1897 was spent in Lojo, where his mother-in-law owned a small estate. Here the ballad *Koskenlaskijan Morsiamet (The Ferryman's Brides)*, for voice and orchestra, was composed, fascinating in its rare combination of somber dramatic suffering and delicate lyrical tenderness.

At this time an important change occurred in Sibelius's life. After the first performance of *Kullervo* voices were raised in the newspapers urging that by means of a public grant the young composer should be enabled to devote himself entirely to his creative work. The Senate turned a favorable ear to the request and allowed him an annual Government grant of 2,000 marks (about 400 dollars).

It is curious to see how the decision of the Finnish Government is regarded in his book on Sibelius by Mr. Cecil Gray, brought up in a country where artists

SIBELIUS AT THE AGE OF FORTY

are not spoilt by encouragement in this form on the part of the ruling Government.

" Such a generous and enlightened gesture on the part of a government towards a young artist must be wellnigh unique in modern times, and deserves every praise. It must be admitted, however, that there are certain risks attached to such a well-meaning course of action, removing as it does one of the most powerful incentives there are to creative activity, namely, the disagreeable necessity of earning a living. Many artists, and by no means always the least gifted — rather the opposite — are notoriously indolent and unable to work save under the pressure of stern necessity. Our own Dr. Johnson, it may be remembered, on receiving a similar pension from the government of his day, practically ceased to do anything at all for the rest of his life except talk. That it should thus have led indirectly to Boswell's *Life* was a fortunate coincidence which can hardly be expected to occur again.

" While as a general rule, then, the practical wisdom of thus generously subsidizing the artist seems very doubtful, the consequences in the particular case in question more than justified the action of the Finnish government. So far from impairing the composer's creative urge it seems rather to have stimulated it, and the vastness of Sibelius's output — greater, perhaps, than that of any other living composer — is undoubtedly due in part at least to the fact that he has been able to give his entire time and energy to the writing of music instead of having to teach or play some instrument in public for a living, or to engage in even more unproductive occupations, as most of his less fortunate colleagues are compelled to do."

Gray is undoubtedly right in saying that Sibelius more than justified the encouragement he received from the Government; he certainly did not follow in the excellent Dr. Johnson's footsteps. On two other points, however, the English critic is mistaken. Official intervention in favor of Sibelius was not quite so unique in the relations between the Government and the world of culture in Finland as Gray assumes, nor did the intervention of the Government enable Sibelius to devote himself entirely to composing. Sibelius was the first musician whom the Government favored in this way, but this procedure was repeated soon after in the case of other musicians and has been adopted to an appreciable extent to the present day. Nor was the Government grant so generously apportioned that, at a time when his international fame was not yet sufficient to ensure him a regular income from his compositions, Sibelius could have entirely given up the additional income he derived from teaching. He resigned his position as teacher in the musical academy only at the beginning of the new century, and even later he

guided a favored few of his talented pupils. Nevertheless, the importance of the Government's intervention
should not be minimized for that reason. During his
last years as a regular teacher at the musical academy
Sibelius was able to restrict his duties, so that they did
not encroach on his own composing to the same extent as before, and if he subsequently went in for teaching, he did so principally out of interest in the development of a younger generation of composers, not with
a view to material requital. In any case the action of
the Government relieved Sibelius of his most burden-
some pedagogic duties — that it is only fair to acknowledge: it afforded him considerable relief and consequently attained its object.

This narrative would be incomplete if all mention
were avoided of a form of activity which, though of
subsidiary importance against the background of Sibelius's real life-work, claimed his time and attention
for many years of his life. It is all the more necessary
to dwell for a time on Sibelius's activities as a teacher,
seeing that he revealed features that are very characteristic of him both as an artist and as a personality.
Sibelius as a teacher is remembered gratefully by
those who enjoyed the advantage of benefiting by his
instruction. In regard to the first phase of his work
as a teacher we have a witness in the composer Otto

Kotilainen, who was admitted to the musical academy as a pupil in the autumn of 1892. Thus Kotilainen's first steps coincided with Sibelius's beginnings as a teacher. Kotilainen says:

" In the theory of music and composition my teachers were the famous principal of the musical academy, Martin Wegelius, and Jean Sibelius. Wegelius, an exacting gentleman of the old school, was a strict disciplinarian whose red pencil and dry, gentle question: 'What is this, M. Kotilainen?' were provoking, though at the same time instructive. Sibelius, whose recently performed powerful musical drama *Kullervo* had caused a tumult in the whole musical world of Helsingfors, was a teacher of a different stamp. It would, of course, be incorrect to say that he did not stick to the rules at all, but he was in no case an adherent of strict style. If the notes and harmonies sounded well and the whole impression was good, he often confined himself merely to mentioning the rules and in this way expressed his approval of the pupil's individuality. ' I myself have had to battle with strict rules,' he said once during a lesson.

" I still retain a vivid recollection of my first lesson in theory at the musical academy. The Finnish-speaking pupils' little extra theory class — two girls from Eastern Finland, like myself, and I — was installed in a room next to the office. I don't know in what mood

the girls, who had already had a few lessons, awaited
the appearance of the teacher. But I was full of excitement, for I had not seen the young master, except when
he conducted the performance of *Kullervo* with the
leader's baton in his hand. The door opened and a
tall, slender man with sparkling eyes and bushy hair
came hurrying in. This was our teacher. He greeted
us, sat down, got up again, lit a cigar, looked out of
the window, cast a quick glance at us three disciples,
and said to the girls: ' It is so lovely outside. Would
you care to take a walk in the fresh air and look at the
town?' And the girls surrendered with joy in their
hearts. ' It would be a pity,' he said, when they had
gone, ' if the young ladies' cheeks were to lose their
beautiful country color,' and smiled a characteristic,
beguiling roguish smile.

" Left to ourselves, the teacher began to examine me
in the general theory of music — which was to be the
subject of our lessons during the whole term. We
ploughed our way hither and yon through Martin
Wegelius's *General Theory of Music and Analysis*,
with its notes, intervals, harmonies, passing notes. We
listened to overtones. He raised the lid of the piano,
pressed the pedal, and struck a low note hard. And
then we listened intently with eyes and ears. ' In the
country I have sometimes heard overtones from a rye
field, as I dozed on the edge of the field,' said my

teacher. I nodded as a sign that I believed him. He even found time during the lesson to explain a little about instruments.

"My teacher walked about for a time and smoked. 'Have you studied harmony?' 'Yes, I have done so — by myself,' I replied. And as I had the book with me, he marked a large number of practice examples from different chapters, told me to solve them, rushed out of the room, and went off into town. About an hour later he returned and by that time I had solved almost all of them. He looked through them with furrowed brow, remarked in some places that the part-writing would have been better in such and such a way, but was also correct as it was.

"I have dwelt on my first lesson at such length — it probably lasted about three hours altogether — because in a way it was my entrance examination as Sibelius's pupil. It was a regular blizzard of theory and afterwards we did not occupy ourselves with the general theory of music as an actual subject. While the girls struggled with the first principles, I began very quietly to do harmony during these lessons and later even counterpoint, and so it went on when I continued my studies with Sibelius at the orchestral school after I had finished the so-called obligatory subjects at the musical academy.

"In the orchestral school," Kotilainen continues,

" I began, in addition to harmony and counterpoint, to work at composition, at first for chorus and solo voices, later small pieces for orchestra. All this time Sibelius was my teacher. My mind rejoices and is warmed to this day when I recall those lessons. How he filled his pupil with enthusiasm and gave him courage, to say nothing of how exactly right his criticism and advice always were! In going through my compositions he never used an instrument, but read them — with the well-known furrows in his brow — and when he got to the end he pointed out the weak parts that had to be corrected by the next time. In addition to the regular lessons in the orchestral school I often visited him in his own home. In connection with these extra lessons I especially remember the time when Sibelius and his family lived at Mattila, near Kervo station, north of Helsingfors. I used to go there throughout a whole winter, sometimes almost every week. As a rule the master sat at his writing-table enveloped in a cloud of smoke from a fat cigar, wrestling with his compositions, with the sheets of the score scattered all over the table. He never indicated by the slightest expression that I had come at an awkward time, but dropped his work and welcomed me."

So far Kotilainen. The portrait he draws of Sibelius as a teacher is supplemented by the narrative of a representative of a younger generation, Leevi Madetoja, who was almost twenty years younger and studied with Sibelius during 1908–10. Like Kotilainen, Madetoja describes his impressions, in *Aulos*, a volume published in honor of Sibelius's sixtieth birthday.

" Sibelius's pedagogic work," Madetoja says, " is a small detail in his life, so rich in creative power; he himself probably considers it unimportant, and it is quite natural that Sibelius the teacher has disappeared entirely in the public consciousness in the shadow of the gigantic figure of Sibelius the composer. It is therefore all the more appropriate on the threshold of the master's birthday to touch on this side of his activities too, with all the more reason as its significance, if we extend the meaning of the word ' teacher,' is greater than we are inclined to think at a superficial glance."

In regard to Sibelius's first years as a teacher Madetoja relies on the oral tradition of the beginning of the 1890's. All that Madetoja collected pointed to Sibelius's lessons having been uncommonly interesting and lively. The statements of Madetoja's informants are completely in accord with Kotilainen's. " Now and then he forgot his pupils, lost himself in his own realms, and at such times it happened occasionally that he let off his whole class. But it is certain that he made manifold recompense for such ' omissions ' by his descriptions, clear and full of imagery, which opened fresh vistas to receptive pupils and appealed to their artistic instincts."

The greatest interest attaches to what Madetoja has to tell us from his own experience about Sibelius as a teacher of more advanced pupils. "I am a bad teacher," were Sibelius's first words, when Madetoja showed him a five-part fugue in his first lesson. "A bad teacher!" Madetoja exclaims and continues: "Well, yes, who is a good teacher and who a bad one? This probably depends in most cases on the extent to which reciprocity is achieved between master and pupil. And I must say that even my first short visit to the master enriched me very much. No instruction in the ordinary pedagogic sense, but short, striking remarks. We did not waste much time on the fugue I had written; we passed on to discuss general musical and æsthetic problems. I remember to this day a good and always appropriate piece of advice in this first lesson: ' No dead notes. Every note must live! ' Is it possible to give a musical student better guidance? Another important aspect of Sibelius's teaching was that he spurred on his pupil to exert his powers. ' You must jump into the water if you are to learn to swim. You must not be afraid of the difficulty of the task; get on with your work smartly and with gay courage! ' I remember many winter evenings when I walked, full of holy enthusiasm and great plans, from Sibelius's house along the Järvenpää road to the station, firmly determined to 'learn to swim.'

"General musical education was thus more characteristic of Sibelius's teaching than the stressing of narrow professional views. And in this sense he has truly been and is still a teacher of all our composers. Principally, of course, of those who have had the good fortune of coming into personal contact with him and who must all, surely, have much to tell of their own experiences in this respect. Sibelius possesses a special gift of giving form to what he says. Only an image, like hitting the nail on the head, and the matter is illustrated more clearly than if a long lecture had been given on it. And nothing in the sphere of music is alien to him. He always finds the kernel, whether it be 'the old' or 'the new' style, or the musical experiments of recent times."

The power of opening a pupil's eyes to the soul of music and of infecting him with his own enthusiasm, of explaining his meaning in short, striking expressions; further, psychological perception of the individual qualities in the pupil's temperament and gifts and a degree of tact that prevents his surrendering to a crippling feeling of inferiority and consequent fear of expressing himself: with these qualities Sibelius has as a teacher already given his pupils more than most creative artists of his rank, whose weakness can generally not be said to have consisted in an unconquerable desire to pass on the experiences and dearly purchased wisdom they have acquired in the exacting struggle with their art.

XIV

THE END OF A
CENTURY

The King Christian suite — A journey to Berlin —
Sibelius finds his first foreign publishers — Sibelius'
first symphony — Beginning of the Bobrikoff régime
— The Song of the Athenians — "Press Celebrations" 1899 — Finlandia — Off to the World Exhibition in Paris.

SIBELIUS worked at almost a feverish pace during
the next few years. His inspiration flowed, ideas
succeeded one another at a rapid rate. During the
remaining years to the end of the century many of the
works were composed that were found most frequently
in the concert programs during the first phase of Sibelius's conquest of the musical world abroad.

At the end of 1897 and the beginning of 1898 the
music for the drama *King Christian II*, the unhappy
King of Denmark, was composed. Sibelius was able

in this case to requite the interest that his friend Adolf
Paul, the author of the play, had taken in him during
his childhood and period of development. He por-
trayed the moods of the drama in four compositions
— four musical poems of fine melodic beauty: " Elé-
gie," " Menuet," " Musette," and the " Fool's Song."

King Christian II was performed for the first time on
February 24, 1898, and the music was played under
the leadership of the composer.

" Immediately after the first night of King Christian," Sibelius relates, " I obtained leave of absence
from my lessons and traveled to Berlin with my wife.
I wanted to hear the new things that were being performed in the outer world, besides which I had many
schemes that I wanted to think over quietly. Former
journeys abroad had taught me that life in large cities
was at times favorable to my composing. To live in a
large city has always been like living in the desert of
Sahara for me. You disappear in the crowd and can
concentrate on yourself."

During the spring in Berlin the musical poem Sandels for male chorus and orchestra appeared — a festal
paraphrase of Runeberg's stirring poem.

Work on Sandels was interrupted by a trip to Leipzig
that Sibelius made in the company of Adolf Paul with
a view to finding a publisher for the music of King
Christian II. The driving force of the expedition was

Adolf Paul, who considered the moment very propitious for making a start among the German publishers. Sibelius himself was much less confident, especially as the attack was to be launched against the almost two-hundred-year-old house of Breitkopf & Härtel, the leading publishers in Germany. His fears proved groundless, however, as the contract was duly signed.

Sibelius still has a lively recollection of the journey and of his first meeting with a great European publisher. His description of his impressions excellently characterizes his behavior in situations in which he had to convert the fruit of his spirit into gold.

" On arriving in Leipzig we hired a cab and gave the driver Breitkopf & Härtel's address. After a time the cab stopped in front of an enormous building — the offices of the great publishers. We entered and were taken charge of by a hall porter, whom we told to announce us. The porter carried out the order and returned with the news that the audience was granted. We were led through one large room after another. Everything made a solemn and awe-inspiring impression. Paul seemed to feel very much at home in these surroundings — it looked as if his hopes grew, the nearer the decisive moment approached. Our progress through the huge rooms had just the opposite effect on me. My confidence decreased at every step I took, and when at last we came into the holy of holies, the manager's room, where the head of the firm, O. von Haase, sat enthroned at a monumental desk under Beethoven's autograph portrait, I was almost ready to sell my compositions for nothing. I was so impressed by the antiquity and traditions of the firm and the awe-inspiring surroundings in general."

The summer found Sibelius and his wife reunited with their children in Lojo. Here Sibelius enriched the music of the *King Christian* drama by three more parts — " Nocturne," " Serenade," and " Ballad."

In the autumn Sibelius moved with his family to Kervo, where he settled down at first in a country house close to the railway station and later in Mattila manor, which was his home during a winter that was as notable in the history of Sibelius's work as the winter in Lovisa after his return from Vienna.

In Mattila Sibelius completed his first symphony. The E minor symphony proved the crowning pinnacle of the period in Sibelius's creative work — we might, perhaps, call it the romantic-realistic period — that was inaugurated by *Kullervo*. But between *Kullervo* and the new work there was a substantial difference.

In *Kullervo* and its successors in the orchestral productions of the '90's Sibelius had composed as a favored exponent of forms and moods with which he was familiar and which set his feelings and imagina-

147

tion in motion: however intensely he felt what he was describing, however fully he entered into the dream-pictures of his inspiration, he had, nevertheless, composed as an onlooker, sympathizing, enraptured.

In the first symphony he identified himself with his work. Here he stepped forth unmasked before the world. It was his own ego he confessed in sound — his dreams, his melancholy, his longing, his undaunted acceptance of life, his indomitable will to assert himself. The heroically tragic feeling of the symphony, its constantly recurring keynote of defiant manly attitude towards existence, misled many of his contemporaries to interpret it as a symbolical image of Finland's readiness to resist the threat from the east. This interpretation was intelligible in view of the circumstances of the time, but it did not go to the heart of the matter. The symphony was something more than that. It was first and foremost a profound human document. It described the struggle of a soul full of conflict for its salvation. It communicated to the world its composer's self-searching — a résumé of what had been and a view of a heavily clouded horizon: it proclaimed his sound resolution to accept whatever fate had in store for him.

The symphony received its baptism of fire before a Finnish audience at Sibelius's concert of his own compositions on April 26, 1899.

148

On the same occasion another work was performed for the first time that turned the concert into something other than a purely artistic event: the *Song of the Athenians* for a combined chorus of boys and men to the accompaniment of a septet of horns and percussion. As characteristic evidence of Sibelius's horror of initiating inquisitive humanity in advance into the secrets of his compositions it may be mentioned that the largest Helsingfors newspaper was able on the very day of the concert to please its readers with the enlightening comment that the program included " a new composition of the talented composer, a symphony in four movements, in the last movement of which a chorus of men and boys performs Viktor Rydberg's *Song of the Athenians*." The work was, of course, an entirely independent one.

The *Song of the Athenians* was the first of the series of antique-like musical poems in which Sibelius, in view of cognate features in his own mentality, confirmed and developed by means of an early awakened passion for the poets of antiquity, was able with ingeniously simple means to give form to the moods and the view of life that flourished on the soil of the gods. But at the same time it was something different.

Finland was going through the first year of passive resistance. Bobrikoff had been Governor-General of Finland for eight months and had during that short space of time exposed the extent of the large Pan-Slavonic plan of attack, of which he was a clever and unscrupulous guardian. The Russian General Staff had aimed an annihilating blow at the Finnish system of conscription; the February manifesto had upset the foundations of the whole legislature. The deputation of five hundred that was to present the great national address was repulsed by the Autocrat of Russia in a humiliating manner. The fight against free speech had flared up with fresh vigor. Embitterment seethed among all classes of the population. Finns and Swedes were united in their determination to resist the Russian assault to the uttermost. The leading Finnish men of culture were actively engaged abroad in their successful mission of combining the representatives of international civilization in a powerful expression of opinion in favor of the little country. Finland strained her powers defiantly in expectation of great events, the issue of which no one could foresee.

In the Song of the Athenians Sibelius gave his people the war-song it required, with an aggressive steely tone not heard in former patriotic songs. The Song of the Athenians admitted without restriction the political interpretation that people were inclined to give the first symphony both then and later. And it is the political background that explains the burning enthusiasm that Sibelius aroused when, in the Song of the Athenians,

SIBELIUS AT HIS WRITING-TABLE IN JÄRVENPÄÄ, 1912

he made the metallic sound of the boys' voices proclaim the readiness of a whole nation to fight and die
for its liberty. A member of the audience at the memorable concert on April 26, 1899 assures us that no
composition of Sibelius carried away the audience to
such a degree at its first performance as the stirring
music to Rydberg's classic verses. At one blow Sibelius had stepped into a leading position in Finland's
political front in virtue of his ability to interpret in
music the thought and purposes that could not be expressed freely in words during the years of oppression.
His place in the consciousness of his people, established by his musical interpretation of forms and moods
of its mythical and historical past, was given an increased and fuller purport by his placing his gifts at the
service of contemporary problems.

The *Song of the Athenians* was Sibelius's first contribution to strengthening the national self-confidence.
It was not long before he was able to make a new one.

During the summer of 1899 the Russian régime of
violence swept with greater force over Finland. It was
chiefly free speech that experienced the displeasure of
the authorities. The watchful Russian officials and
their helpers among the submissive elements in Finland were untiring in their zeal. One newspaper after
another was forced to be silent. Suppression, either
permanent or temporary, was the fate of most of the

patriotic newspapers of the country, no matter whether Finnish or Swedish, large or small.

In the autumn of 1899 the people of Finland decided to show their appreciation of the most open champions of Finland's rights and constitution in that phase of the struggle. The patriotic demonstration took the form of fêtes, lotteries, and entertainments in aid of the press pensions fund. The idea was enthusiastically supported throughout the country, all classes took part, and the " Press Celebrations " on the 3rd, 4th, and 5th of November provided a rich pecuniary and spiritual harvest. The celebrations in Helsingfors culminated in a gala night in the Swedish theater on the 4th of November. The principal item in the program consisted of a series of " Tableaux from the Past " staged by Kaarlo Bergbom, the manager of the Finnish national theater, and provided with suitable words by Eino Leino and Jalmari Finne. There were six tableaux and their contents were indicated by the following wording in the program:

I. *Väinämöinen Delights Nature, the Kalevala and Pohjola People by His Songs.*
II. *The Baptism of the Finnish People.*
III. *From Duke Johan's Court.*
IV. *The Finns in the Thirty Years' War.*
V. *During the Great Troubles.*
VI. *Finland Awakes.*

The taste of the expiring '90's for historical tableaux, rather unintelligible for us, was unabated and Bergbom's production was loudly applauded by the crowded audience. The truly artistic contribution consisted undoubtedly of Sibelius's music to the series of tableaux, although according to contemporary critics it did not attain its full effect in its original setting. The music comprised an overture to the whole series, an introduction to each tableau, and a concluding musical poem, besides a soft accompaniment to the words.

Just as Sibelius's tableau music in the earlier '90's was far from being superficially illustrative, the music for " Tableaux from the Past " only came into its own when it was performed independently in the concert hall in the strict selection the composer had made in the suite *Scènes Historiques I*, consisting of three numbers: " All' Overtura," " Scena," " Festivo."

The most striking music that Sibelius composed for the " Press Celebrations " of 1899 was not included in the *Scènes Historiques*. This was the finale. Neither the critics nor the public grasped at first what it expressed. The realization of this only awoke when, after a thorough revision, it was given the name that informed the whole world that close to the Arctic Circle a small nation was struggling for its existence. This name was *Finlandia*.

" It was actually rather late," Sibelius recalls, " that

Finlandia was performed under its final title. At the farewell concert of the Philharmonic Orchestra before leaving for Paris, when the tone-poem was played for the first time in its revised form, it was called *Suomi*. It was introduced by the same name in Scandinavia; in German towns it was called *Vaterland*, and in Paris *La Patrie*. In Finland its performance was forbidden during the years of unrest, and in other parts of the Empire it was not allowed to be played under any name that in any way indicated its patriotic character. When I conducted in Reval and Riga by invitation in the summer of 1904, I had to call it *Impromptu*."

Finlandia represents Sibelius's second great direct contribution to the work of political resistance in Finland at the end of last century. In spite of its national tone the tone-poem has gained such world-wide popularity that, as Sibelius's English biographer expresses it, " it is in the repertory of every orchestra and every brass band." It has, perhaps, not been entirely an advantage to the appreciation of Sibelius as a composer that his name was for a long time connected almost exclusively with *Finlandia* in the minds of many people abroad. For Finland his composition was of undoubted benefit. In the efforts to convince the world that Finland was something other than a number of governments under the scepter of the Autocrat of Russia, *Finlandia* was of greater significance in its day than hundreds of pamphlets and newspaper articles.

The portrait of Jean Sibelius during the last years of the nineteenth century would not be complete if mention were omitted of some works that throw light on his feelings and ideas.

Several other of the songs that have established his fame as a composer of songs refer to 1899, a year exceptionally rich in fruitful spiritual experiences. The throbbing, painfully curbed passion in " Black Roses," the nobly resigned melancholy in " But My Bird is Long in Homing," the realistic characterization in " Tennis at Trianon," the pure poetry in " March Snow " — what proof of the sincerity and wealth of his lyrical inspiration!

In the autumn of 1899, a couple of weeks before the " Press Celebrations," the Savo-Karelian student corporation was able to come out in the program of its evening entertainment with a recitation to the accompaniment of chorus and orchestra, *The Breaking Up of the Ice on the Uleå River*, in which the painter of nature speaks again. In the first months of the new century *Snöfrid* appeared, in which Sibelius gave life to the enchanted atmosphere of Rydberg's poem in music in an intensified, brilliant, and sterling form.

Sibelius was now thirty-four years old. He had established a unique position in his own country, but he was not well known abroad. Excepting for sporadic performances of small orchestral pieces in Germany, his work had not been introduced to the public in the leading musical countries.

Karl Flodin, constantly an interested observer of the Sibelius phenomenon, describes the position in his book *Finnish Musicians*, published in the spring of 1900: " Sibelius is not only Finland's first and, so far, only composer of genius, but the equal, as regards the great qualities of a composer, of poets of the highest rank in all countries, who write in music. It is really high time that Sibelius's best work should be known beyond the confines of his own country. Sooner or later this is, indeed, bound to happen, for whatever is excellent, original, and ingenious must finally burst the bonds imposed by unfavorable conditions. And genius belongs to the world. . . . The most national of all modern composers, Grieg, has long since gained the rights of international citizenship. It should now be Sibelius's turn."

And Flodin added these words that so acutely predicted the conclusion that Sibelius was himself to come to after the experience of several decades:

" But in reality he composes for at least a generation ahead. His music is such that the general musical sense of the public must be extraordinarily developed for this music to be understood at once and to become popular in the ordinary sense of the word. As regards momentary success this is, of course, unfavorable, but for the fame and understanding of Sibelius in the future it is only an advantage — if this is of any comfort to the composer, who would, no doubt, prefer to be understood and appreciated during his lifetime."

The introduction to the world outside Finland actually occurred sooner than Flodin, perhaps, expected when he wrote the lines quoted. In the late winter of 1900 it was decided that the orchestra of the Philharmonic Society should visit the Paris Exhibition in order that, in addition to Finnish architecture and painting, the rapidly advancing music of Finland should bear witness before foreign countries of the vitality and originality of Finnish culture at a time when this was of special importance for political reasons. As the government refused to contribute towards the expenses, a fund was collected privately, sufficient to ensure the success of the undertaking at any rate on a modest scale. On July 1 the "Paris Tour of the Philharmonic Orchestra" gave its first farewell concert in Helsingfors; on July 2 its second. On the following day it started for its campaign on the continent of Europe. The journey included Stockholm, Oslo, Göteborg, Malmö, Copenhagen, Lübeck, Hamburg, Berlin, Amsterdam, Rotterdam, Brussels, and Paris, where the tour ended with two concerts on July 30 and August 3. The principal items in the program consisted of orchestral works by Sibelius, Järnefelt, and Kajanus. Finnish folk-songs and vocal music were sung by Ida Ekman, who accompanied the orchestra as soloist, and at the concerts in Paris Finnish song was also interpreted by Aino Ackté and Maikki Järnefelt. Sibelius was worthily represented in the orchestral program by the first symphony, the *King Christian* suite, the two *Kalevala* legends, and *Finlandia*. On the other hand, Sibelius as a composer of songs was not officially represented during the tour except at one concert in Brussels.

Sibelius accompanied the tour as assistant conductor, but did not have an opportunity of performing his works personally. His part was confined to coming forward and receiving ovations, and in many cases he did not even do that. For him personally the tour proved a pleasure trip, with plenty of experiences and amusing episodes. For his work the tour was a triumphal procession. The testimony of the critics is incontestable. His special position among Finnish and northern composers was acknowledged unanimously by experts in the musical capitals. His unique gifts and originality aroused delight and wonder. He was acclaimed everywhere as a rising star.

"The Paris tour was, on the whole, a pleasant and refreshing experience. I made many interesting acquaintances during it. On our visit to Stockholm I met the Swedish composer Hugo Alfvén. He struck me as a profound and philosophical character and particularly attractive as a man. In Paris I became acquainted with old Johan Svendsen, who was at that time court conductor in the Danish capital. He was very delighted with my music and promised to do his utmost to make it better known in Denmark. He was particularly struck by my first symphony. He eagerly urged me to take steps to get it printed."

The Paris journey was the first stage of the conquering march of Sibelius's music through Europe. It was soon to be succeeded by fresh successes. Such an art as Sibelius possessed, owing to its special character and originality, was highly calculated to make its mark in a world in which vital music represented a tiny fraction of the mass of imitative art and works of cold, intellectual experimenting. Against the background of this fact it was of minor importance in the long run that Sibelius himself was animated by the sincerest disinclination to advertise his art and establish personal connections purely with a view to the advantage he could gain from them.

"My attitude has never been an active one when there was a question of clearing the way for my music," Sibelius himself confesses. "I have always preferred to let my works speak for me."

159

XV

THE YEARS OF

COLLECTING

*An important stay in Berlin — In Italy — Meeting
with Anton Dvořák — Musical Festival in Heidelberg
— Sibelius as a conductor — The second symphony —
The Origin of Fire — Back in Berlin — Felix Weingartner.*

ΒN the autumn of 1900 Sibelius made a long journey abroad. Having made arrangements for a
deputy to take his place at the musical academy and
orchestral school, he started for abroad with his family
at the end of October.

He first set his course for Berlin, where he stayed for
several months. His sojourn in the German capital
was of decisive importance in acquainting Sibelius with
the musical world of Germany. Chance came to his
aid in this.

In connection with a Dvořák concert in the large

Philharmonic Hall, Otto Lessmann, the influential publisher of the *Allgemeine Musikzeitung*, arranged a reception in his private house at which some of Germany's greatest musical celebrities, such as Richard Strauss and Felix Weingartner, were present. A Finnish lady singer had appeared as a soloist in the Dvořák concert and she succeeded in persuading her reluctant fellow-countryman to attend the reception, at which an extensive musical program was performed. Sibelius was even persuaded, under urgent pressure, to agree to a selection of his songs, including "The Tryst," composed in Berlin, being performed before the exacting audience of rival composers and other experts.

The proof of his art that was given in this way evoked lively approval among those present, and the radiations of Sibelius's lively and unique personality made the more thoughtful ones realize that this soul contained still richer treasures of artistic invention and creative power. Before the company broke up, Sibelius had acquired some good German friends, among whom Otto Lessmann was not the least enthusiastic, and a few weeks later Sibelius was informed that he had been included in the list of composers for the coming musical festival in Heidelberg of the Allgemeiner Deutscher Musikverein.

This important association of musicians, founded

forty years before by Franz Liszt, was then controlled almost autocratically by Richard Strauss, who was not famed for favoring composers who acknowledged other ideals than his own. That Sibelius, so unlike the post-Wagner tendency in temperament and technique, should have been singled out by the mighty " Richard II " was all the more remarkable seeing that previously only two northern composers had been invited to the general German musical festivals: namely, Edvard Grieg and Christian Sinding.

Encouraged by this pleasing news, Sibelius moved on with his family at the end of February 1901 to Rapallo.

" The beginning of our stay," Sibelius recalls, " was anything but agreeable. We had rain, cold, and wind. The local inhabitants declared that they had not had such a bitter winter within the memory of man. It is easy to imagine what it felt like to wake up in the morning with six degrees of frost in the room; it was impossible to heat, because the rooms had no stoves.

" At the beginning of March the weather grew milder and I was able to enjoy the beautiful scenery to the full in one of the loveliest parts of Italy. It was the season for violets — the woods were filled with their scent. I used to take long walks from the town of Rapallo along the hills on the shore covered with pines, olive trees, and cypresses, to Zoagli, Santa Marguerita, Santa Miguela, and Portofino. The blue sunny Mediterranean lay bordered by the most luxuriant flora.

"In Rapallo my family lived in the Pension Suisse; for myself I rented a workroom in a little villa in the hills, surrounded by a most interesting garden — roses in bloom, camellias, almond trees, cactuses, agaves, magnolias, cypresses, vines, palms, and quantities of flowers."

Free from the troubles of daily life, Sibelius was able to devote himself entirely to composing.

"Now I am again completely a man of imagination," he writes in a private letter of March 6. "Nothing disturbs me. I could initiate you, my comprehending friend, into my work, but I do not do it from principle. To my mind it is the same with compositions as with butterflies: once you touch them, their essence is gone — they can fly, it is true, but are no longer so fair."

The work that was written during the Italian spring was the radiant second symphony — a spiritual confession like the first, but of a brighter temperament, in which melancholy was interpreted in more controlled expressions, and strong outbursts were softened by a more optimistic outlook on life and a joyful feeling of the delight of creating, a work of wide horizons with light and power in it.

At the beginning of May, Sibelius and his family started for home.

" On our way north I stopped in Prague, where I met the excellent Bohemian musician Joseph Suk, whose acquaintance I had made in Berlin. Suk had married a daughter of Anton Dvořák and he introduced me to his father-in-law.

" I was not able to spend much time with Dvořák, but it was sufficient to give me an extraordinarily favorable impression of him. The old man was naturalness and modesty personified and spoke very modestly of his art, not at all as one would have imagined from his position in the musical life of his country and of the world. Incidentally, he said quite sincerely: ' Wissen Sie, ich habe zuviel komponiert (Do you know, I have composed too much) .' I could not agree with his opinion."

After a short stay in Finland the hour of departure again struck for Sibelius. The date of the musical festival in Heidelberg, June 1–4, was approaching. It had been agreed that he should personally conduct his works that had been accepted for performance: " The Swan of Tuonela " and " The Return of Lemminkäinen."

The thirty-seventh musical festival of the Allgemeiner Deutscher Musikverein provided no less than five concerts and a gala performance in the Court

THE SIBELIUS FAMILY AT JÄRVENPÄÄ, 1916

Theater in Karlsruhe. The majority of the items in the programs were new, performed by the composers themselves, and the audiences consisted almost exclusively of experts and celebrities in the musical world.

" My position as a foreigner among a crowd of German composers with big names and influence was no easy one. It was not surprising that the organizers were chiefly concerned with giving a worthy performance of the German celebrities' long compositions, which, superficially, seemed much more difficult to play than mine. Apart from the dress rehearsal on the morning of the day of the concert I was only allowed one rehearsal for works that were quite strange to the German musicians both in spirit and in style. At this first rehearsal everything went wrong and the dress rehearsal was not much better. As, besides, everyone was tortured and irritated by having to work in intolerable heat — during the whole of the musical festival it was over eighty degrees in the shade — you will understand that I looked forward to the combined performance of the orchestra and myself at the concert with a good deal of anxiety."

But the evening came and at once all was changed. We must call upon Adolf Paul, who was present in Heidelberg and watched the fate of his friend with anxiety and excitement and hastened to report the final victory in a letter home.

" Sibelius displayed such energy and mastery that I was simply astounded; the orchestra obeyed his slightest sign and formed an ensemble that allowed both the glorious tone-poems to make their full effect felt. Some slight unevenness was, of course, unavoidable, but it did not matter and was not noticed. The spiritual contents received full justice, the audience was moved by the poetic beauty of both the legends and readily became enthusiastic. It was new and original, it was fresh and independent, ingenious and brilliantly done, and, above all, it was no imitative music. Sibelius was recalled several times by tumultuous applause and was complimented *coram publico* and behind the scenes by a great number of celebrities. The reporters nodded and looked pleased, old Lessmann, who is an enthusiastic admirer of Sibelius's art, was moved and proud. Hermann Wolff at once fixed a date for a Sibelius concert in Berlin. In short, people's eyes were opened to the fact that this new man was indeed a great figure and that the name of Sibelius was one of the few round which the greatest hopes of the music of the future would center.

" The greatest significance of his appearance in Heidelberg for himself is, no doubt, that he has discovered a new feature among his gifts. And not only that, but that it has been implicitly acknowledged.

" For he is no more and no less than a very unusual

166

conductor. And one of that rare kind that is not only able to enter into and render plastically and clearly the works of art he presents, but that, above all, irresistibly subjects both orchestra and audience to the power of his personality, turns them into one heart and one soul, combines them into one great intoxication of rapture, and makes them as ready to receive as he is to give. If, then, you have something to give, your triumph is assured. It was this quality that broke forth in Sibelius in his hour of need and led him to victory in spite of all, and when ordinary conductors' tricks would certainly have broken down for want of rehearsals."

His appearance in Heidelberg undoubtedly proved a brilliant victory. Those who may be inclined to ascribe Adolf Paul's enthusiastic description partly to friendship will find it confirmed by another eyewitness, the Nestor among Finnish musicians, old Professor Richard Faltin, who also witnessed Sibelius's appearance in Heidelberg and gives an account of the event in a letter to his wife:

" In spite of many adverse circumstances, which I will describe orally, Sibelius has scored a great success. His compositions were, strictly speaking, the last item in the endlessly long program, for after them only Wagner's *Kaisermarsch* was played, which has for years formed the official conclusion of these musical festivals. This time the audience joined in singing the

hymn *Heil dem Kaiser* in unison for the first time, as
Wagner wanted it. You can imagine how wonderful
it was! Before Sibelius in the program came Richard
Strauss with two big songs with orchestra. You see
that Sibelius's position was not an easy one: between
Strauss, whom the orchestra greeted with a threefold
fanfare, and the audience by rising, and Wagner. Besides, we had already heard over three hours' music in
truly tropical heat! Sibelius was recalled twice, a success that weighs all the more in the scales in view of the
adverse circumstances I have referred to."

The musical festival in Heidelberg is a pleasant
memory for Sibelius. " It meant much for making my
art known in Germany, and I was surprised by the kindness and cordiality I received on all hands. I remember
in particular the occasions on which I spoke with Richard Strauss, who was busily occupied during the whole
of the musical festival. He was extraordinarily amiable
to me and spoke very frankly of his works. I was much
pleased that the difference in our conception of art did
not form an obstacle to our excellent personal relations.
In later years, too, I was able to convince myself that
he regarded my art with an impartiality and loyalty
that I was bound to appreciate very highly."

From Heidelberg Sibelius returned home with his
family. For the remaining part of the summer he settled in Lojo, where he stayed until late in the autumn

and worked with seething inspiration to complete the second symphony.

In October Sibelius again moved to Kervo. He was no longer tied by his duties as teacher at the musical academy.

" I was now able to devote myself entirely to composing. I devoted all my strength to completing my new symphony. By the end of the year the work was ready."

The D major symphony was performed at Sibelius's concert of his own compositions on March 8, 1902. At the same time another novelty was performed, *Impromptu*, for women's chorus and orchestra, to words by Viktor Rydberg, Sibelius's second inspired act of homage to the world of antiquity.

Soon after, Sibelius was ready to appear before the public with yet another work: *The Origin of Fire*, for baritone, chorus, and orchestra.

" The piece was composed for the inauguration of the new Finnish theater on April 9, 1902, and was played on that occasion under my leadership with the help of the Philharmonic Orchestra and a chorus of 350 people. It was a memorable night. The main item of the program, as regards acting, was Alexis Kivi's *Lea*, in which Ida Aalberg played the leading part with all the supreme art that distinguished her. I was very pleased with the performance of my own composition.

169

It was intended for sound and breadth, and I thought that it sounded well."

"Later in the spring," Sibelius continues, " I went to Berlin. During my stay there in the previous year Arthur Nikisch, the great leader of the Philharmonic Orchestra, had grown interested in my music and had, among other things, spoken of performing ' The Swan of Tuonela.' I called on him in order to show him some new works, but found him remarkably changed. I had a feeling that people had been intriguing against me and this proved to be the case. I remember how one of my German musical friends tried to comfort me by saying: ' *Lieber Freund, jetzt bist du erst vollständig anerkannt wo die Intriguen anfangen* (My friend, now you are thoroughly recognized, seeing that the intrigues are beginning) .'

"From Felix Weingartner, on the contrary, I had a thoroughly friendly reception. I had already met him fleetingly the year before and was now able to renew our slight acquaintance.

"He made an extraordinarily attractive impression on me. There was something so noble and personal about him. He begged to be allowed to keep the score of my second symphony in order to study it more closely, and promised, after going through it carefully, to send it on to Breitkopf & Härtel, who had undertaken to print it."

170

XVI

THE YEARS OF
CHANGE

*The summer of 1902 — Valse Triste composed —
The violin concerto — Wilhelm Stenhammar — An
internal crisis — Sibelius decides to leave Helsingfors
— The feeling in the spring of 1904 — The home in
Järvenpää completed.*

N June 1902 Sibelius was in Finland once more.
The longing for sea-air forced him to settle for
a few weeks in Tvärminne. Here " Was it a Dream? "
one of the noblest products of Sibelius's lyric inspiration, was composed, followed by " Autumn Night,"
" On a Balcony by the Sea," and other beautiful songs.
The composer of songs was going through a busy period, foreshadowed in the spring by " Berceuse " and
" Sunrise."

In the autumn Sibelius settled down in Helsingfors.
Here he composed the music for his brother-in-law

Arvid Järnefelt's drama *Kuolema* early in 1903. It included *Valse Triste*.

" I composed *Valse Triste* originally for string orchestra. The composition with all retouching was finished in a week. Later I scored it for a small orchestra."
Sibelius declines to say more about a work the fascination of which is certainly not based on such cheap qualities as one might be tempted to believe in view of its exceptional popularity all over the world.

By the violin concerto, which he completed in its first version during the summer of 1903, Sibelius solved another hard problem: the composition of a virtuoso piece that at the same time satisfied all the demands regarding style bound to be made of a symphonic work. The violin concerto was given its final shape two years later, in the summer of 1905, when it appeared in the form in which it attracts present-day violinists with technical and at the same time artistic pretensions.

In the autumn of 1903 Sibelius's second symphony was performed in Stockholm. Among those present was the excellent Swedish musician Wilhelm Stenhammar. Some time later he sent Sibelius a letter, dated Saltsjöbaden, January 4, 1904. The letter is indicative of the honored position already given to Sibelius by responsible musical opinion and at the same time expresses a hope shared by many:

172

It is already a long time since we heard your symphony here; I thought of writing on the following day, but failed to do so, and so I put it off. But you must have a few lines. For you must know that you are in my thoughts daily since I heard the symphony. You wonderful man, it is indeed a large catch of marvels that you have brought up out of the depths of the unconscious and the inexpressible. What I suspected has come true: at this moment you are to me the foremost, the only, the unfathomable. And I only await now your appearance before the world in a clear and tangible form — give humanity hope, give us the drama! You do not need it; I, too, can dispense with it; but all the many who now turn away from a riddle they cannot solve, they require it. Lift up the forms from your wonderful Finnish world of legend, set them forth as great simple symbols of all the mystically deep that you can never express by anything but music, but can also never explain in any other way than by action. I beg this of you for the sake of all those who unconsciously long for it.

I have also written a symphony now. At any rate it is called a symphony. And by an agreement that you may have forgotten, it was to be dedicated to you. Nothing has come of it, however. It is quite good, but is superficial. I long to go into myself. And you must wait until I have got there. On the great day on which that happens I will place your name in capitals on the title page, whether it be a symphony or anything else. Until then I carry your name faithfully and reverently in my grateful

173

soul, where it will remain for all time. You have stirred
me so much that I cannot forget it.
Your friend,
Wilh. Stenhammar

"My acquaintance with Wilhelm Stenhammar,"
Sibelius relates, "dates from a visit he paid to Helsingfors in February 1902. We discovered each other from
the first moment. In him I found an understanding of
my art with which I was not spoilt in Scandinavia when
the century was young; and when I subsequently
turned into paths along which many of my former
adherents found it difficult to accompany me, I had the
unaltered support of Stenhammar. As the leader of the
Göteborg Orchestral Society he was always ready to
champion my cause — at that time the only Swedish
musician in a prominent position of whom I can say
that. In later years we often met during my visits to
Sweden, and I always found his friendship for me undiminished. A rare friend — an uncommonly noble personality, a genuine and intelligent musician, and a gentleman from top to toe."

The winter of 1903–4 was spent by Sibelius and his
family again in Helsingfors.

Sibelius was approaching an inner transformation, a
crisis that was to leave deep scars on his soul.

The *Sturm und Drang* period of his youth and early

174

manhood was over. Physical causes had contributed their share: an affection of the ears that had begun in 1901 and was only completely cured in 1905 made him apprehensive of total deafness in his hours of depression. But the essential part of the process was played out in the secret depths of his soul. Life changed its countenance for him. Moods of titanic defiance, of suffering melancholy and arrogant acceptance of life no longer held solitary sway in his soul. Life set him new problems, raised his feelings and views to a more noble, more spiritual plane. His wrestlings with new problems, during which he was thoroughly misunderstood by most of those around him, created a feeling of isolation that plunged him into melancholy at times, but the piercing acuteness of which at the same time and to an even greater degree steeled him.

The man and the artist were one in him. In the case of such a thoroughly honest and conscientious artist as he was, spiritual experiences had of necessity to be reflected in his work to force him away from spheres already tested, in which he could have gained fresh, easily won laurels, and to guide his searching spirit into ways where fresh victories could only be gained by fresh struggles. This honesty towards himself was bound to create a gulf between him and his audience, but he was willing to pay the price. If his artistic career during the following years became in many respects

175

a martyrdom, the martyrdom was at any rate of his own choosing. He had chosen his fate open-eyed. He could not jest with his genius.

The second symphony had already given warning of a new artistic and human faith, a flight from elemental passion and intensity of feeling towards clearness, moderation, and balance. This tendency was to appear still more clearly during the years that lay before him. While his contemporaries endeavored to instill fresh vigor into their composing by a more extended use of the technical means of musical art, by strengthening the orchestral apparatus by introducing new and astonishing instruments, while the younger generation was engaged in seeking new sound-values in the labyrinth of the atonic scales, Sibelius's art moved towards the deepening and simplifying that enabled him to grasp the hands of the classics across the gulf of centuries. The first monumental proof of this process having been successfully accomplished was the third symphony.

The spiritual transformation evoked a longing for new surroundings. Helsingfors had no fruitful influence on his creative work. The experiences of the past years had taught him that his art demanded that he should live either in the country in Finland or in some large city on the Continent. His life in Helsingfors in 1902–3 and 1903–4 confirmed this. These two winters were comparatively barren of new works in comparison with the abundantly productive years about the turn of the century. In the spring of 1904 Sibelius finally decided to move into the country. He says of this:

" It was necessary for me to get away from Helsingfors. My art demanded another environment. In Helsingfors all melody died within me. Besides, I was too sociable to be able to refuse invitations that interfered with my work. I found it very difficult to say no. I had to get away."

Once the decision had been made, a country house was bought in Tomasby near the Tusby Fens, about two miles from Järvenpää railway station north of Helsingfors.

Sibelius's last spring in Helsingfors was distinguished by the hopeful mood aroused among the inhabitants of the capital by the Russo-Japanese War. Events in the Far East were followed with breathless attention. We catch glimpses of them in Sibelius's correspondence — for instance, in the following temperamental outburst on March 8, 1904:

" What do you say about the war? The official reports!

" Japan has twenty-three warships and, according to Bobrikoff, forty have been destroyed! *Sic itur ad Gehennam!* "

The new house in the country, however, occupied Sibelius's thoughts most. All the arrangements, including questions of finance that were necessary for building the villa, gave him much food for thought. In the middle of March he was able to write to a friend: " The villa has a stone foundation and five tiers of logs. I wish I could get it put up! I fight for it tooth and nail. I long for peace and quietness. And to be able to work without worry."

Sibelius spent the summer of 1904 with his family in a farmhouse in Tomasby in order to watch the building of the villa at close quarters. Two series of concerts in Reval and Riga, whither he had been invited by his fellow-countryman Georg Schnéevoigt, formed a refreshing change. The concerts were, of course, not important occasions, but the orchestra — the Warsaw Symphony Orchestra conducted by Schnée-voigt — was first class, and at that time Sibelius seized every opportunity of conducting his works in person.

" It was at these concerts," says Sibelius, " that I conducted *Finlandia* under the title of *Impromptu*. Political conditions necessitated this farce, but the greater part of the audience, no doubt, understood what it was about. In any case the nationality of the composer could not be concealed and the ovations I received might, perhaps, be interpreted to some extent as expressions of sympathy for our country. In Reval

178

the concert was attended by many naval officers, who sent me their cards after the concert with expressions of thanks. Among their names I noticed a large number that sounded Finnish."

In the meantime the building of the villa proceeded and in September the house was ready to receive its tenants. Sibelius moved into the house that was to afford him comfort and protection through life's varying changes and has remained his home to the present day. He had realized one of the main conditions of the continuance of his creative work.

The effect was soon apparent. A letter dated September 21, 1904 closed with the laconic but significant remark:

" Have begun my third symphony."

XVII

CONQUESTS IN

EUROPE

The Busoni concert in Berlin — Toscanini — The death of Albert Edelfelt — Sibelius's first visit to England — Paris — The death of Martin Wegelius.

HE YEAR 1905 proved an important year in the slow but irresistible conquest of the foreign musical world by Sibelius's music. The composer in Järvenpää established contact with the great centers of music that fortified him during a trying period of his life and gave him encouragement that he was in great need of from a purely human point of view.

"In January 1905 I was summoned to Berlin by Busoni in order to conduct personally the performance of the second symphony at one of the concerts in the 'Moderne Musik' series."

His appearance in Berlin was a complete success. We turn to Adolf Paul again, who tells the Finnish

180

public about the triumphs of the friend of his youth.

" This year people speak of the Busoni concerts bare-headed, express unqualified approval of their good object and of the self-sacrifice of their organizer, who has, unfortunately, not yet achieved the success of being able to present anything really vital.

" Then came the last concert and with it Sibelius's second symphony. It was like setting a match to gunpowder. I have seldom seen such enthusiasm as on its conclusion. Proper ovations to Sibelius from both the orchestra and the audience. Time after time he was called out to receive the applause of the audience. I need not tell the Finnish public how he conducted his work. But the Philharmonic Orchestra played it brilliantly, with swing, fire, and enthusiasm. It was a success that not only gave Sibelius a firm position here, but also provided excellent evidence of the justification and necessity for Busoni's orchestral concerts.

" ' Busoni's concert nights are among Berlin's most interesting concert undertakings,' the Welt am Montag writes suddenly. And another paper, the National-Zeitung, says expressly of Sibelius's second symphony: ' a work that it was the duty of Nikisch or Weingartner to let us hear.'

" In general the press notices are brilliant. The Tageblatt and Lokalanzeiger, indeed, qualify their approval with some far-fetched ifs and buts of no significance. But all the rest of the press, including the great newspapers published outside Berlin (*Kölnische Zeitung*, for instance) report the triumph, draw attention to Sibelius's absolute mastery in handling the orchestra, his lively imagination and inventive powers, and the brilliancy and swing and the rousing strength he was able to display, especially in the two last movements of the symphony."

After his success in Berlin, Sibelius came home with the intention of soon going abroad again, for in the previous summer he had received an invitation to conduct his first symphony in Liverpool and Manchester, and the concerts had been fixed for March.

" I had looked forward to my journey to England with great expectations. Busoni had spoken many times with rapture of England and had praised its audiences as remarkably receptive to anything new in music, and I had made a solemn vow to myself: I shall go there! The concerts in Liverpool and Birmingham were to come off in March and I had already made all my arrangements for the journey when I was prevented at the last moment and had to telegraph a refusal. My compositions were played under the leadership of Granville Bantock, who had conducted both my symphonies before.

" Bantock played the first symphony, *Finlandia* and the *King Christian* suite, and to judge by the critiques

182

JEAN SIBELIUS

they were very successful. I noticed then already that Englishmen understood certain features in my music that were dismissed by the German critics of that time as mere mannerisms."

At about the same time a couple of Sibelius's works had their first performance in Italy. It was none other than Arturo Toscanini who played *Finlandia* and *The Swan of Tuonela* with the La Scala orchestra of 120 musicians.

" Since then Toscanini has shown a gratifying interest in my music. A few years ago he performed my fourth symphony in New York. The work did not have a very warm reception, which is not surprising at its first performance, but in order to hammer it thoroughly into the consciousness of the staggered public Toscanini played it at the next three consecutive concerts. But it is only a conductor of Toscanini's unique position who can allow himself such a thing."

While his works were going from triumph to triumph abroad, Sibelius worked on assiduously in his country seclusion. During the spring of 1905 the music for Maeterlinck's drama *Pelléas and Mélisande* was written, approaching pure music in its dreamy beauty as closely as is possible in the case of music for a play.

In August 1905 Sibelius had to perform the painful duty of writing funeral music for Albert Edelfelt's burial. The music was written for a mixed choir to Runeberg's moving words: "Not with lament shall thy memory be honored," and the choir was led by the composer at the solemn service in the Church of St. Nicholas.

"In October 1905 my violin concerto, in its revised and final form, stood its baptism of fire in Germany at a concert in the Singakademie in Berlin. The solo part was played by Carl Halir and the accompaniment was conducted by none other than Richard Strauss. As an instance of Strauss's extraordinary conscientiousness in performing the works of other contemporary composers, it should be mentioned that he had three rehearsals with the orchestra for practicing the accompaniment. But the violin concerto requires it."

A month later Sibelius was at last able to realize his plan of visiting England. He was invited to Liverpool to conduct the second symphony, but was determined to spend a few weeks in England in order to study conditions there. He had received invitations from many quarters.

"During the early part of my stay in England I lived at Granville Bantock's, who owned a splendid country house near Birmingham. In his house I enjoyed true English hospitality — so great that I did not become acquainted with the English coins.

"Then I went to London. Here I was taken charge

of by Sir Henry Wood and met many people who subsequently did a great deal to make my music better
known in England, among them Mrs. Rosa Newmarch
and Ernest Newman, who has followed my production with close attention and whose analyses of my
personality as an artist, marked by his intellect, with
its many facets, have always interested me.

"I liked England very much. It was an indescribable joy to me to see ancient, special culture at every
step, based on the respect for the power of traditions,
which appealed to me very strongly.

"I immediately discovered the error in the very general impression current at that time that Englishmen
have no natural talent for music. On the contrary, they
are very capable musicians, although in their splendid
isolation they do not trouble to advertise themselves.

"During my first visit to England Hans Richter, my
old acquaintance of the Court Opera in Vienna, was
still conducting in Manchester, where not long before
he had successfully performed my first and second symphonies. I had no opportunity of meeting him personally, but received a friendly greeting from him,
which pleased me very much.

"Before I left London an agreement was come to
with Sir Henry Wood for a performance during the
following year, and I had already been engaged for Liverpool, Birmingham, and Manchester. I was not able

to carry out these plans — my personal début before a London audience did not come off until two years later, but my works occupied a favored place from that time in the program of Wood's orchestra. As early as February 1906 he performed the *Pelléas and Mélisande* suite. Since then he has often championed my music and has been quick to perform new works of mine. I enjoyed the same kindness in all respects from his wife, a woman of quality and an excellent singer.

" In later years Great Britain came to signify more and more in confirming the position of my art in the international world of music. I have been fortunate in gaining many new friends. I need only mention the name of Sir Thomas Beecham to give an idea of the keen understanding that the musical life of Britain has shown for my art."

From London Sibelius went over to Paris in the middle of December.

" I lived in historic surroundings during my short visit to France, in Saint-Germain, Pavillon Henri IV — an environment that has a very inspiring influence on me. From my windows, I had a splendid view of the whole of Paris and its surroundings. I came to France in a happy hour. I was able to convince myself that of late my works had been performed very frequently in Paris and that I was a composer who was talked of. A month before Chevillard, leading the Lamoureux orchestra, had played the *Swan of Tuonela*, and *Finlandia* was on the program of one of the next concerts of the orchestra. During my stay in Paris I had several opportunities of noticing the respect Frenchmen showed for the Legion of Honor that I had been awarded in 1903."

In January 1906 Sibelius returned to Finland. His scheme of work was fully drawn up. The third symphony, which he had worked on a great deal in Paris, awaited completion. The music for his friend Hjalmar Procopé's play, *Belshazar's Feast*, which was shortly to have its first night, was an urgent task. In addition Sibelius was inspired once more by a subject from the *Kalevala*, *Pohjola's Daughter*, which was the origin of a symphonic fantasy for a large orchestra.

In the midst of all this the news reached him of Martin Wegelius's death on March 22, 1906. The cultural life of Finland had suffered another irreparable loss within little more than six months. The news was not unexpected — the state of Martin Wegelius's health had for some months given warning of the unavoidable end.

Sibelius felt keenly the loss of a friend who had stood by him loyally for twenty years, who had witnessed and encouraged the union of the youth of twenty with the art of music and had watched his development with undiminished interest and goodwill, even when he could not quite understand the novelty and pioneer-dom in his work. Among the musical honors at Martin Wegelius's funeral the "Elegy" from the *King Christian* suite was played, under the leadership of the composer.

XVIII

EVENTFUL YEARS

The third symphony — Gustav Mahler in Helsingfors — Svanevit (Swanwhite) — Second visit to London — Miss Mary Wakefield — Reception in Oxford — Operation in Berlin — Voces Intimæ — Back in London — Journey to Koli — Night-ride and Sunrise.

SIBELIUS's creative work proceeded at an even pace.

The *Belshazar* suite was ready by the date fixed and in the autumn *Pohjola's Daughter* was completed, the first performance taking place under the leadership of the composer in St. Petersburg shortly before Christmas 1906, at a Siloti concert.

On March 17, 1907, Sibelius was invited to conduct the performance of his new symphony in London. The invitation was sent by the famous Royal Philharmonic Society, and Sibelius expressed his satisfaction in a letter:

" The invitation to London was a great honor. It

will be strange to stand on the same spot where everyone from Haydn to Tchaikovsky has performed his
works."

Sibelius was obliged to postpone his appearance in
London, however. The third symphony ripened
slowly. The master's incorruptible self-criticism performed its work of selection and improvement.

During the summer of 1907 the C major symphony
was finished. On September 25 Sibelius arranged a
concert of his own compositions, after an interval of
two and a half years, at which the new symphony was
performed as well as *Pohjola's Daughter* and the *Belshazar* suite. The three works, composed during the
same period, were a brilliant testimony to the exuber-
ant wealth of Sibelius's art: the wealth of shifting
colors and the splendid orchestration in *Pohjola's
Daughter*, the Oriental coloring achieved by simple
means in the *Belshazar* suite, the noble, great joy, the
classical moderation, and the bright clearness in the
third symphony.

Some time after the concert, Sibelius made one of
the most remarkable acquaintanceships in his life.
Gustav Mahler had started on his victorious progress
through Europe shortly before his brilliant American
period and also visited Helsingfors, where the audience
was able to hear him at a concert on November 1, 1907.
During the time that Mahler stayed in Helsingfors this

peculiar Austrian composer came into close contact
with Sibelius.

"Mahler and I spent much time in each other's
company. Mahler's grave heart-trouble forced him to
lead an ascetic life and he was not fond of dinners and
banquets. Contact was established between us in
some walks, during which we discussed all the great
questions of music thoroughly.

"When our conversation touched on the essence
of symphony, I said that I admired its severity and style
and the profound logic that created an inner connection between all the motifs. This was the experience
I had come to in composing. Mahler's opinion was
just the reverse.

"'Nein, die Symphonie muss sein wie die Welt.
Sie muss alles umfassen. (No, symphony must be like
the world. It must embrace everything.)'

"Personally, Mahler was very modest. He had
heard that the Gambrinus restaurant was a popular
resort of orchestral musicians and spoke of dining
there. When I suggested that a Mahler ought, perhaps, to visit a higher-class restaurant, he replied
curtly: 'Ich geh' wohin ich will (I shall go where I
please).'

"A very interesting person. I respected him as a personality, his ethically exalted qualities as a man and an
artist, in spite of his ideas on art being different from

mine. I did not wish him to think that I had only looked him up in order to get him interested in my compositions. When he asked me in his abrupt way:

" ' *Was wollen Sie dass ich von Ihnen dirigiere?* (What would you like me to conduct of yours?) ' I therefore only answered:

" ' *Nichts* (Nothing) .' "

Sibelius was faced with a fresh task. Strindberg's fairy-tale *Swanwhite* was to be produced in Helsingfors in the spring of 1908 and the management of the Swedish theater succeeded in persuading Sibelius to write the music.

" The task attracted me very much. Strindberg, who essayed so many things, had thought of writing the music for the play himself. When he heard that I had undertaken the task, he gave up his work. He informed me of this in a letter that I still keep. A year later I revised the music for *Swanwhite* thoroughly. From this the suite appeared that is played at concerts."

On February 20, 1908 Sibelius went to London to conduct his new symphony at the Philharmonic Society. A long-cherished wish was thus fulfilled.

" My second visit to London proved even more productive than the first. I improved my acquaintance with old friends and made new ones.

" Among others I met Miss Mary Wakefield, who had been a close friend of Ruskin's and Grieg's and was an outstanding personality in the musical life of England.

" A good singer in her youth, she had devoted her wealth and interests to far-reaching musical plans. In various English towns she had established choral societies, which met annually in order to perform works for choir and orchestra from Bach to present-day composers in accordance with her guiding principle: ' to bring the greatest music within reach of the greatest numbers.' My *The Captive Queen*, too, was included in the program of these musical festivals. She was close on sixty when we became acquainted, and had already retired from the active management of her musical festivals, but still exercised a great influence. A very unusual woman, lively and interesting. An acquaintance certainly worth making."

The language obstacle presented some difficulty, but did not prevent mutual understanding.

" They met several times," Mrs. Rosa Newmarch, who introduced them to each other, relates, " and although neither could speak more than a few words of any language that the other understood, they succeeded in understanding something of their mutual opinions and convictions about art. Sibelius' songs, with their exalted idealism and subtle reflection of nature, found a profound response in Mary Wakefield. How she would have sung them twenty years earlier! "

193

" During my second visit to England," Sibelius continues, " I also attended a reception in Oxford that had been organized by my friends in London. I arrived in the venerable university town on the previous evening in the most wonderful moonlight. In this magic light Oxford reminded me in a strange way of Venice. The ceremony itself made a profound impression on me. I have seldom felt so impressed."

After his pleasant stay in England Sibelius returned to Finland. He had to face a trial of a grave nature.

For a long time he had been suffering from an affection of the throat that caused him serious concern for the future. Physicians had not been able to establish the nature of the trouble. Cancer was feared, but it was not certain. After undergoing an unsuccessful operation in Helsingfors in May 1908, Sibelius went to Berlin on the advice of his doctors.

" I was advised to consult the greatest specialist in Europe, Professor X. He examined me carefully and found that it was not cancer, but a malicious tumor that could, however, be removed by an operation. For a couple of weeks in June 1908 I underwent treatment from him that was both trying to my patience and painful. The professor was already an old man, yet he was, nevertheless, determined to remove the cause of the trouble with his own hand. I was obliged to submit to thirteen operations on my throat without any result. Finally the old man gave it up and handed the operation over to his assistant, a young man with sharp features and a steely look, the personification of ability and energy. He lowered his instrument into my throat and found the bad place. A strong jerk, a shout of triumph: '*Jetzt hab' ich's!* (*Now I've got it!*)' — and he pulled out the instrument. I was released from torture.

"After the operation the doctors could not be certain for a long time whether the trouble would not recur and possibly develop into the illness they feared. For many years I had to exercise the greatest care and, for instance, give up cigars altogether, which meant a great sacrifice. It was only during the World War that I gradually took to smoking cigars again, without its doing me any harm."

Anxiety as to his fate depressed Sibelius very much at times during these and many subsequent years. Worries of other kinds, including financial anxiety, that it would have been easier to bear when he was younger, but, of course, were hard to bear for a man of Sibelius's age, also cast a dark shadow over his life.

Sibelius's letters prove this. There are passages that are very significant in their restrained brevity; for instance:

"I do not advise anyone without private means to become a composer. That way lies tragedy. . . ."

But grim humor breaks out as frequently:

" Astronomy is certainly the best antidote for business worries. . . .

" 2,000 light years!

" 2,000 marks to pay to the bank — "

And then this passage:

" Do you go in for money lotteries? I am bombarded with lottery catalogues. It is said to be a sure sign of imminent ruin. A juicy list of prizes lies before me. A million. Well — well."

While Sibelius had in his youth devoted himself to the worship of the difficult art of chamber music, he had during the following couple of decades moved exclusively in other spheres. The orchestral and song composer had forced himself so much into the public eye that it had almost been forgotten that his originality and special gifts had first been revealed in works in the field of chamber music.

When in December 1908 Sibelius started to write a string quartet the forty-three-year-old master began where the youth of twenty-four left off; what crowding moods and memories of the past this must have evoked from his soul in comparing and explaining the present moment!

His thoughts are reflected in a letter written about this time to a close friend:

" I see by your letters that you are living in the past

and in your childhood. As a matter of fact, I believe that such spiritual baths are a necessity to the soul. We become aware of the guiding principle of our lives and understand it better.

" Now that I have calmed down I can get a true insight into my life and my art, and I find that steady pressing forward and progress are possible to me and the only thing satisfactory. Unmusical Goethe has, perhaps, expressed the greatest musical truths in his Sprüche. And during this time he has given me backbone.

" Much could be said about this. . . ."

What Sibelius could not put into words he expressed in music. Voces Intimæ was the title of the quartet — this reveals more than enough of its character, a work full of the reflections and doubts of its author. It is a mature man who sums up his experiences in it, not a youthfully defiant iconoclast; there are ten years between Voces Intimæ and the first symphony. The work does not say anything definite; its author's work is not yet finished; he still has a long road to travel and he knows it. The work fixes a point in his development, moods and thoughts on one stage of the journey in its subdued, mysterious keynote.

Voces Intimæ was completed during a stay in London during February–March 1909: the analogy with the winter of 1889–90 in Berlin, when the G minor quintet appeared, strikes the eye. While Sibelius was writing in the turmoil of a metropolis a work that was, of all his compositions, one of the furthest removed from the tumult of the world, he did not lose contact with the world surrounding him.

" On February 12 I conducted a concert in Queen's Hall which proved a great success, to judge by the attitude of the critics and audience. During my stay

Facsimile of the opening bars of Voces Intimæ in a private letter dated December 15, 1908

in London Debussy and Vincent d'Indy were also staying there and I made their acquaintance. I received much kindness from my English friends and was invited to a great number of dinners which I enjoyed very much, although I was not allowed to touch either wine or cigars. I found that the new régime benefited my composing. It was only when I dispensed with all narcotics that I found I could think and feel with real intensity. I heard a lot of new music: Elgar's new symphony, Bantock's *Omar Khayyám*, Debussy's new songs and his orchestral suite *Nocturnes* — very interesting music. All I heard confirmed my idea of the road I had traveled and had to travel."

It seemed as though the self-confession in *Voces Intimæ* had released fresh powers in Sibelius's inner being. When he left London at the end of March 1909, his head was full of new ideas. The remaining two months of spring were spent in intensive work in Paris and Berlin, where the eight songs to poems by Josephson, glowing with intense feeling, were written. The composer's inspiration flowed with undiminished strength after he had returned to his own country. Sibelius was working on no less than three works simultaneously: the tone-poem *Night-ride and Sunrise*, a funeral march for large orchestra, and the music for Mikael Lybeck's play *The Lizard*. Besides, he found time for minor pieces, such as two songs to the guitar from Shakspere's *Twelfth Night* and ten pieces for piano subsequently published as opus 58.

The summer of 1909 was a season of work, with little contact with the outer world. The news that filtered through from it to the master's inviolable home in Järvenpää was of a mixed nature. It was very pleasing for him to hear that his works were now proceeding from triumph to triumph in America. Now and then he also received critiques from Europe that made him conscious of his art still having to experience skepticism and opposition on its path. But the master no longer allowed this to disturb his equanimity.

" I had gradually schooled myself to the experience of being beset daily by the musical press of the world and being given reminders of good and bad. I had taught myself to take attacks fairly calmly. I was now so sure of my art. If I read critiques of devilish asperity, I took it as a proof of my development proceeding *ad astra.*"

Sibelius expresses the same thought in a letter of that time:

" I am now fairly immune from vulgar attacks. They are generally stupid and my anger does not last long. Bad critiques actually have a refreshing influence on me. Almost humorous. I am really like old violins that sound better the more mended holes they have."

Early in October 1909 Sibelius set off with his brother-in-law Eero Järnefelt on a trip to the Koli hills in Karelia, on the western shore of Lake Pielisjärvi, to the same district that he had once visited, seventeen years before, as a bridegroom. Järnefelt had been to Koli before during the days of sound and joy of national romanticism, but to Sibelius Koli was something new.

The whole journey took a week; the stay on the Koli

peninsula, where they arrived by water late at night, lasted twenty-four hours, and their stay on the hills themselves only occupied a couple of hours, but it proved an unforgettable experience. While Eero Järnefelt worked at his easel, Jean Sibelius stood patiently beside him, smoked a cigar — in spite of doctor's orders — and thoroughly enjoyed the magnificent view. It was a wonderful day. The wind sang; it was bitterly cold. At one moment the sun would shine on the two artists with a cold sparkling light, the next they were exposed to hailstorms and strong gusts of wind. Wherever they turned their gaze they found inspiring impressions: autumnal Pielisjärvi with its bluish-gray waves, whose turbulent play was enlivened from time to time by a splash of sunshine, the cold, white cliffs, the scarred landscape round the hill, the view towards the Russian frontier across a limitless sea of forest, finally the wild vegetation in their rambles in the gloaming, while descending to the little lake of Herajärvi in the southwest, across the moonlit waves of which the travelers had themselves rowed in order to make for the nearest railway station on the opposite shore.

Jean Sibelius, the worshipper of nature, was the richer by a great experience. His experiences on the trip deeply affected the continued process of spiritual change under the power of which he was still living. They gave his creative spirit fruitful impulses in its unceasing pursuit of fresh beauties of clearness and perfection.

Immediately after his return from Koli Sibelius proceeded to put the finishing touches to the music for *The Lizard*. The task was finished on the night of October 15. At that stage of his development Sibelius estimated this work, unfortunately not yet published, very highly. In a letter of that time he describes the music for *The Lizard* as " among the most full of feeling that I have written."

In a letter written a few weeks later he reveals his feeling to a close friend:

" I have great plans. I think you will soon be able to convince yourself that my art will gradually seem convincing and ' cheerful.' "

The labors of the summer were drawing to an end.

" *Night-ride and Sunrise* was completed in November 1909. A month later I finished the funeral march. I did not want to call it ' Marche Funèbre.' Some time later I hit upon its title: *In Memoriam*. The title may give the impression that I was thinking of the death of some particular person when I wrote it. This is not the case, however.

" The idea of both *Night-ride and Sunrise* and *In*

Memoriam came to me a long time before. The principal motif of *Night-ride* was conceived during the spring in Italy in 1901, when I made a trip to Rome in April. The motif of *In Memoriam* occurred to me in Berlin in 1905."

XIX

TOWARDS CLARITY
AND PERFECTION

*The composing of the fourth symphony — Storm
clouds in the east — The concert on April 3, 1911 —
In Berlin and Paris — Offer of a professorship in
Vienna — Concert tour in England — Invitation to
America.*

IN the spring of 1910 Sibelius started work on
the new symphony that was to occupy such an
important place in the history of his life and work.
During the whole summer of 1910 he was wrapped in
the mysteries of artistic production. He experienced,
as he confesses in a private letter, hours of creative
anguish more sublime than ever before.

It was a hard time for his country. After a few
years of armed neutrality the Russian attack on Finland's rights and constitution had been renewed with
fresh vigor. Stolypin's proposals of Imperial legislation that subordinated the most essential questions

connected with Finnish economic, cultural, and political life to the decision of the Russian authorities
had been passed by the Russian Duma by a vast majority. Pourishkevich had triumphantly proclaimed his
famous "*Finis Finlandiæ!*" The protests of the European world of culture had, as ten years before, remained unheeded by the spokesmen of the policy of
Pan-Slavonic expansion in St. Petersburg. The Russian power was preparing for a decisive move against
Finland. The position was more threatening than it
ever had been.

References to the threatening political situation occur frequently in Sibelius's letters of this period. He
watched the terrifying course of events with gloomy
foreboding, but did not try to find forgetfulness and
relief from his anxiety in fruitless theoretical arguments.

"Politics have never interested me in themselves.
That is to say — all empty talk on political questions,
all amateurish politicizing I have always hated. I have
tried to make my contribution in another way."

In this sense, too, we must understand an expression in a letter written in August, 1910, at the time
that the Finnish Diet was considering its attitude towards the projects of Imperial legislation received from
St. Petersburg.

"Politics do not interest me at present. For I cannot help in any other way than by laboring ' for king and country.' I am working on my new symphony."

The symphony governs the whole of Sibelius's life. Glimpses of it appear incessantly in his letters, in words that make us suspect what a struggle the new vein he is introducing into his composition is costing him. He works at it while staying in Oslo in the beginning of October, in pursuance of an invitation to conduct a concert of his own works. He works at it in Berlin and Leipzig, which he visits at the end of the month.

Here is a triumphant conclusion to a Järvenpää letter in December 1910:

" The symphony is breaking forth in sunshine and strength."

Sibelius was also occupied with other things at this time. In January 1911 he composed two orchestral pieces, " sisters of *Valse Triste* ": *Valse Romantique*, for a small orchestra, and *Canzonetta*, for string orchestra. But the symphony was the main task that was nearest his heart.

The slowly maturing score of the fourth symphony accompanied him when he started in February 1911 on a concert tour embracing Göteborg, Riga, and Libau, during which he also made a trip to Berlin.

On his return to Finland the new work was finished: the fourth symphony in A minor, throbbing from the first bar to the last with the proud and severe gravity

SIBELIUS AT JÄRVENPÄÄ WITH HIS WIFE AND A DAUGHTER

of a suffering and triumphing being. Like the first symphony, the fourth crowns a phase of the master's production — it spreads the annunciation and immortality of great art over the inner process of change that extends its roots backward to the somber winter of 1903–4.

Before Sibelius presented his new composition to the audiences of Helsingfors he was able to compose another tone-poem for orchestra, the *Dryad*, a new pearl in the string of his antique-like tone-poems.

The fourth symphony was performed for the first time at a concert in Helsingfors on April 3, 1911, at the same time as the *Dryad*, *Canzonetta* for string orchestra, *In Memoriam*, and *Night-ride and Sunrise*.

" If *Voces Intimæ* was difficult to understand, the fourth symphony was even more so. An orchestral work, in which nothing was based on utilizing the orchestral resources, in which everything that could appeal directly to the senses and elementary feelings was carefully avoided, in which all was spiritualized beauty, reproduced by the most ascetic means — such a composition gave the Helsingfors audience much to ponder over. The first reception was marked by the hesitation of the audience and critics. The composer was shown all the respect due to him, but people were not sure how they were to understand the latest product of his genius. A critic in one of the leading Helsingfors newspapers found that he could not explain the symphony except by laying down a definite program. He connected the work with the trip to Koli and explained, movement by movement, what landscapes it intended to depict.

Contrary to his custom, Sibelius felt called upon to enter the lists publicly against the critic's interpretation of his work. It was not that he had any wish to deny the significance of possible impressions of nature for his inspiration — a connection between the symphony and his experiences at Koli was indicated by the circumstance, surely not entirely accidental, that the work was dedicated to his companion on the trip, Eero Järnefelt. What he objected to was that impressions from the outer world of reality should be interpreted as decisive in a work that, above all, described experiences of an introspective, spiritual nature, arising from pondering over the most important problems of existence, life and death. It was the tendency to try to find a program basis for a work that was entirely in the realm of pure music that aroused the composer to a protest, laconic, but very indignant.

In the autumn of 1911 Sibelius again made a journey abroad.

" During October I lived in Berlin, during November in Paris. The prolonged concentration on my own art drove me with greater force than ever before to try to gain momentary release from myself in the concert halls. I have never listened to so much music as during those two months in the autumn of 1911. I listened to as much music as I could, both old and new. I have always been interested in contemporary and younger composers as much as anything in order to gain a clear view about myself. In listening to the quantity of modern music with which I then became acquainted, I came to the conclusion that many present-day composers, in their endeavors to preserve their place in the public eye, through constantly having to produce something novel and sensational had lost the power of composing anything living based on the old ecclesiastical scales; this, I thought, was reserved for me and others who could live in greater peace."

No wonder Sibelius generally derived greater benefit from listening to compositions of the older masters. He discovered new beauty in works to which in the critical *Sturm und Drang* period of his youth he had been opposed. The mature master, sure of his work, could freely enjoy beauty wherever he found it, even though it proceeded from other sources of inspiration than his own art. A letter written after a Bruckner performance shows how intensely he could enjoy music:

" Yesterday I heard Bruckner's B major symphony

and it moved me to tears. For a long time afterwards I was completely enraptured. What a strangely profound spirit, formed by religiousness! And this profound religiousness we have abolished in our own country as something no longer in harmony with our time."

At the beginning of 1912 Sibelius was offered a professorship in the Conservatoire in Vienna. The offer was a great distinction, but it did not cost the master a long struggle to decline it.

" My head was too full of my own ideas to allow me with a clear conscience to accept a position which, if it were to be well filled, would have demanded a good deal of time and interest in the work of young talents. Besides, in order to secure the post in Vienna I should obviously have had to undertake to stay a long time in Austria and to become an Austrian subject. And I wanted to remain in my own country! "

By the spring Sibelius had another group of *Scènes Historiques* ready: " The Chase," " Love Song," " At the Drawbridge " — like the first series at the turn of the century, pictures full of color and brilliance from a departed time of chivalry and brave deeds. In the summer the first of the original serenades, opus 69, for violin and orchestra in D major appeared, to be succeeded in the following year by the second in G minor. Three sonatinas for piano also belong to the harvest of 1912.

In the autumn of 1912 Sibelius again made a journey to England.

"This time I was engaged to appear in five towns, Liverpool, Manchester, Birmingham, Bournemouth, and Cheltenham. The principal item in my programs was the fourth symphony and I was very curious as to how it would be received by the English public. The venture was undoubtedly bold in view of the doubtful reception it had had from the public in Finland. The English, however, proved surprisingly sympathetic; nowhere was there such a climax as in Göteborg, where at its first performance the symphony was actually received with hoots."

On returning to Finland Sibelius buried himself during 1913 in the realm of myth in the moving tone-poem *The Bard*, for orchestra, and in the fragile and sensitive tone-poem *Luonnotar*, for soprano and orchestra. Concentration of a different kind was required of him in composing the music for the pantomime *Scaramouche*.

During the last few years Sibelius had had frequent proof of his growing popularity in America. The Americans were anxious not to be behind their Anglo-Saxon brothers in Europe. One organization after another had approached him with a request that he should cross the Atlantic and give the American musical public an opportunity of hearing his own interpretation of works that they had learned to appreciate and love through others.

Sibelius had gratefully but firmly refused these proposals. Indifferent to a high degree throughout his whole life to the material results of his work, he was afraid in the midst of a creative period of rare intensity that the long voyage and the multiplicity of fresh impressions and experiences would hamper the flow of his productive vein in too great a measure.

The autumn of 1913 found him at length more inclined to hearken to the enticing voices from the New World. A wealthy American, Mr. Carl Stoeckel, had approached Sibelius in Järvenpää with a request for a new work for orchestra and had at the same time invited him to conduct this composition and older works at a Sibelius concert at a musical festival in the beginning of June. The American's letter was couched in terms that bore evidence of a personality both rarely appreciative of art and noble, very different from the type of arrogant plutocrats that popular fancy in Europe still pictured at that time as the successful American business man. The personality of the man who had invited him, in conjunction with other fortunate circumstances, induced Sibelius to cease hesitating and decide to cross the Atlantic. He accepted the invitation and at once started on the new work for his American friend.

XX

THE NEW WORLD

*Awarded the degree of doctor at Alexander University
in Helsingfors — Sibelius goes on board the Kaiser
Wilhelm II — The voyage across the Atlantic — Arrival in New York — Musical festival in Norfolk —
Litchfield Choral Union Society — Banquet in Boston — By car to Niagara — Award of degree at Yale
University — The return journey on the President
Grant — News of the Sarajevo murder — A concert
that did not come off.*

AᴛT New Year's, 1914, we find Sibelius in Berlin
working with great inspiration. The German
capital was the external setting of his creative pains,
but his inspiration followed the Attic line in his soul.
The new work that was completed in the spring in
Järvenpää, became a joyous ocean poem, full of life
and sunshine. The title Sibelius thought of originally
was " Vågornas Rondo — Rondo der Wellen." Its
final name was *Oceanides.*

He was now ready for the voyage to the New World.

213

"As the date of my departure approached," said Sibelius, " I received an invitation to have the honorary degree of doctor conferred on me at the Alexander University in Helsingfors at the spring session. This proof of the appreciation of my countrymen at a time when I needed it badly pleased me very much. It hurt me that, while accepting the honor of the invitation, I had to say that I would not be able to be present in person when the degree was awarded. My promise to Mr. Stoeckel was binding in any case, and it would have been all the more difficult for me to go back on it at the last moment, as I knew that extensive arrangements had been made to make my stay in America both productive and pleasant. My friends in Finland fully appreciated my point of view."

On May 16, 1914 Jean Sibelius left Helsingfors to start on his voyage to America via Bremen on the newly built North German Lloyd liner *Kaiser Wilhelm II.*

The voyage across the Atlantic provided Sibelius, the lover of nature and creator of *Oceanides*, with many new sensations.

"The ocean was an unforgettable memory to me. The weather was fine and beautiful throughout the whole voyage except for one day of storm and thunder. I saw many glorious nights on the Atlantic. In particular I remember a sunset that was one of the most enchanting I have ever seen. I have never seen such a high sky arching itself over an almost wine-colored sea — violet and blue clouds, a wonderful combination of color. One morning the sea was quite silver-gray. Its color merged so imperceptibly into the faintly clouded sky that it was impossible to see where the horizon began. Suddenly there was a moving ripple of darker gray in the distance across the smooth, silver-gray field — about fifty porpoises that slowly approached the ship and passed it in a playful row."

On arriving at New York on May 27 Sibelius was met not only by his host, Mr. Stoeckel, but also by reporters from the great daily papers, who assailed him with all the questions that American interviewers are used to showering upon foreign celebrities. Sibelius, who had behaved like a modest first-class passenger among hundreds of others who made far more fuss, realized of a sudden what a great name his actually was in America. This first reception exceeded all his expectations.

" I was quite astounded at being so well known in America. I should never have believed it."

Already on the first day of his stay in the New World Sibelius had weightier proof of the appreciation that he enjoyed. On being comfortably installed in the fashionable New York hotel in which he was to rest after the voyage, he was informed by Mr. Stoeckel that Yale University had decided to confer the honorary degree of Doctor of Music on him on June 19. The matter had been kept strictly secret and Sibelius was requested not to mention anything about it in his letters home to people who might spread the news before the date of the ceremony arrived.

"Yale University," Sibelius explained, "wanted to give me a pleasant surprise by informing me of its decision to confer the honorary degree of doctor on me only on my arrival in America. The decision had been passed on the motion of Professor Horatio Parker, who occupied the chair of music in the university and had for many years been active on behalf of my art. It was a great distinction, for Yale University had awarded very few degrees of Doctor of Music."

On the following day Mr. Stoeckel escorted his Finnish guest to his estate, situated a few hours' railway journey from New York, near the little town of Norfolk, in the northwestern corner of the state of Connecticut. This estate was to be Sibelius's headquarters during his stay in America. As soon as he arrived, he was given an opportunity of conducting his first rehearsal with the orchestra that had been engaged for the musical festival. This already filled him with the brightest hopes in regard to the festival.

"What an orchestra!" Sibelius exclaims, enthusiastic at the very recollection of it. "A hundred splendid musicians selected from the finest performers in the orchestras of Boston and New York: the best orchestra I have ever conducted. Simply glorious! Such chords from the wood wind instruments that you had to put your hand to your ear to hear their pianissimo, and double basses that sang."

All this was calculated to create in Sibelius from the first a festive and expectant mood: the reception, the external frame for his appearance, his hosts. " I really felt in my element," he confesses.

" Mr. Stoeckel, a middle-aged man of Austrian extraction, was a highly cultured personality. His varied interests were shared by his wife, a very pleasant woman, descended from the French Huguenots. Mr. and Mrs. Stoeckel combined the best American and European characteristics in their persons.

" Their wonderful estate lay among wooded hills, intersected by rivers and shimmering streams — the sort of district in which Leatherstocking formerly dwelt and had his being. The shell of the main building was one of the oldest houses raised by white men in America — an exceptionally beautiful creation in the new French style, built by an ancestor of Mrs. Stoeckel's in the eighteenth century. The natural surroundings had not been disturbed, but were reverently protected from the advance of civilization; it was as romantic and

217

mysterious as it had been two hundred years earlier. There was an atmosphere of poetry over the large, sleeping woods that was unique.

"Like so many other wealthy Americans Mr. Stoeckel considered that he should also display some activity on behalf of his cultural interests. His great love was music. This he had inherited from his father, Gustav J. Stoeckel, an Austrian musician, who had immigrated and had for forty years been professor of music at Yale University. The son's ideas on musical questions were in all respects marked by the opinions and taste of a professional musician. Mr. Stoeckel and his wife had had an enormous music room built on their estate, a monumental wooden building in the American ' Colonial ' style, where they arranged a large musical festival annually in conjunction with the Litchfield County Choral Union, an exceedingly distinguished choral society that had only prospered thanks to the generous support of Mr. and Mrs. Stoeckel. No expense was spared to raise the musical festivals to the highest level conceivable; Stoeckel made himself responsible for everything. His noble and broadminded musical culture could be traced in the programs: they included both classical works and what was of value in modern European music and the works of progressive American composers. The musical festivals on Mr. Stoeckel's estate were, therefore, among the most notable events of American musical life, taken note of by all who meant anything in the sphere of music and culture. This was the kind of musical festival in which I was invited to take part."

The Litchfield County Choral Union was so re- markable a phenomenon in " unmusical America " that it deserves to be described in greater detail.

As a souvenir of his visit Sibelius brought back two elegantly bound volumes describing the origin and activities of this undertaking. From these we gather that the Litchfield County Choral Union was founded in 1899 by Mr. and Mrs. Stoeckel in memory of Mrs. Stoeckel's father, Robbins Battell, a man zealous for public welfare, a supporter of art and music and a philanthropist on a large scale, one of the benefactors of Yale University; that the union embraced five small towns in New England — Norfolk, Winsted, Salisbury, Canaan, and Torrington — from among those inhabit- ants of which who were musically intelligent and gifted with voices members were selected for the special choir that performed the principal part in the musical festivals in the month of June. We learn further that these musical festivals were given added brilliance by the appearance of leading vocal and instrumental solo- ists of the New and Old Worlds, and that among the honorary members of the Union, chosen from among composers who had contributed to the programs, there were such celebrities as Anton Dvořák, Camille Saint-Saëns, Max Bruch, and Arrigo Boito.

In the course of time the Norfolk Festival had come to be called by American and European judges "America's Bayreuth." In this connection Mr. Stoeckel had written a letter to the Hartford *Courant* which is reproduced in the memorial volume and gives an excellent conception of his personal views on art and his mentality generally. The following is an extract:

"Bayreuth was founded for the glorification of one man, undoubtedly the greatest genius who ever revealed himself in the composition of opera. As an egoist the twin brother of Carlyle, he could see little or no excellence in the works of other composers, and the fundamental idea of Bayreuth and everything connected with it may be summed up in one name: Wagner. Whatever excellent points Bayreuth may have had during his lifetime, it has lost largely since his death, and the glamour of his name in connection with what is vaguely termed 'atmosphere,' is all that remains to lure curiosity-seekers, rather than artists, to renditions of Wagner's works which would not be tolerated in New York. . . .

"Not the slightest idea of Bayreuth or anything connected with it ever entered the minds of the founders of the Norfolk movement in music. Bayreuth is for opera — comparatively speaking, a rather inferior form of music.

220

The opera has yet to be made which as pure art can be placed on a level with the greater symphonies of Beethoven or equal to the imaginative, pathetic, and sublime choral conceptions of Bach, and to such works Norfolk is and has been committed. . . .

"Bayreuth knows but one composer; at Norfolk all schools and nations have been, and will be, welcome. . . ."

A composer, Mr. Stoeckel continues, who is invited to Norfolk is freely entitled " to create according to his own intentions," to select soloists and have at his disposal as large an orchestra as he wishes and to have as many rehearsals as he considers necessary. He retains all rights in connection with his work and in addition receives a good round fee. " Can we conceive of Bayreuth giving a cash honorarium or parting with its copyrights to any but the Wagner family? "

In the book on the Litchfield County Choral Union it is further pointed out that it is the Union whose duty it is to approach a composer with a request for new works for its musical festivals. " No offers of compositions are, therefore, taken into consideration, seeing that the selection should fall on a composer who has in no way offered his services. This procedure makes it possible for us to address ourselves to artists of the highest rank, and our principle will be only to favour composers whose position is such that they would consider it beneath their dignity to come forward with an offer."

Finally a rule especially calculated to appeal to Sibelius: No publicity is permitted in connection with the concerts, the sole object of which is to honor the composer and his works in the most exalted forms.

No wonder that Sibelius felt happy in surroundings on which such an aristocratic conception of art had set its stamp. He continues his narrative:

" While waiting for the date of the musical festival, Mr. Stoeckel did his utmost to make my days pass in a pleasant manner. He extended hospitality to me that really overpowered me. I was surrounded with everything that the luxury of the American upper classes had to offer. I have never, before or after, lived such a wonderful life. I recall with special regret the cigars that Mr. Stoeckel provided me with, but which I dared not touch for fear of a renewed affection of the throat. What a fool I was at that time! "

On June 3 the sun rose on the first day of the great musical festival. On that day Handel's monumental *Messiah* was performed with the assistance of artists from the Metropolitan Opera House. The third and last day was devoted to modern American music. Between them came the Sibelius concert; thus a whole day was devoted exclusively to Sibelius's music. The program consisted of *Finlandia, Pohjola's Daughter*, the *King Christian* suite, and, as an imposing finale, the new musical poem *Oceanides*.

That day is an unforgettable memory for Sibelius.

"There was such a wonderful festive atmosphere over it all from the moment I came in, when the audience rose and the orchestra joined in with a thundering 'fanfare.' I noticed with emotion that the conductor's desk was decorated with the Finnish and American colors. The audience consisted of close on two thousand guests by invitation — a high-class audience, representative of the best that America possessed among lovers of music, trained musicians, and critics. The most inspiring setting for the appearance of an artist. The concert concluded with the Finnish national anthem, *Vårt Land*, sung to English words by the huge choir to the accompaniment of the orchestra, and with the American national anthem."

The concert proved a complete triumph for Sibelius. The audience greeted his works with thunderous applause and the critics were no less enthusiastic. Krehbiel, one of America's leading critics at that time, wrote:

"During the last fifteen years I have felt three times that I was confronted with a world genius: when Richard Strauss, first with the New York Philharmonic Orchestra and later with the Boston Symphony Orchestra, performed his own compositions; when Arturo Toscanini in 1910 in the Boston Opera House directed an unforgettable performance of ' Tristan and Isolde '; and lastly when, by the courtesy of Mr. Carl Stoeckel, I had the privilege of hearing Jean Sibelius from Finland direct nine of his old and new compositions on June 4th, 1914."

If the musical festival in Norfolk signified a great personal triumph for Sibelius, the latter was, for his part, no less delighted by what he had the opportunity of hearing of the works of others.

" The idea I obtained there of the musical life of America was extraordinarily favorable. I thought it surprisingly rich. The performance of Handel's *Messiah* with the magnificent choir of four hundred male voices and the brilliant soloists was wonderful, fully comparable to the best in Europe. Of the young American music I received a very pleasing impression. In our own country many people at that time still had the idea that American music was exhausted if you mentioned the Boston and ragtime. I was able to convince myself on the spot of the thorough fallacy of such a view. There was much in the work of the young American composers that was built on European models, but also much that indicated that in the realm of music, too, the Americans were pressing forward with well-directed energy towards independent forms. From that moment I realized that American music was

SIBELIUS AT THE PIANO

also a factor to be reckoned with in the musical life of the world."

The musical festival in Norfolk was succeeded by the next great event in Sibelius's sojourn in America, the award of his degree at Yale University. This, as already mentioned, was fixed for June 19. Thus there were two weeks before the event. The attentive Mr. Stoeckel saw to it that the period of waiting was passed in the pleasantest way possible.

" Mr. Stoeckel was untiring in his efforts to make my stay on his delightful estate as pleasant for me as possible. Besides, he arranged trips for me to adjacent towns and places. These trips were made either in a motor car or in a specially reserved Pullman car, and the servants were always sent off in advance to make all preparations, so that one felt at home wherever one went.

" On one of these journeys Boston was visited, where a large dinner was arranged at which I made the acquaintance of practically all the leading composers in America: Chadwick, Hadley, Loeffler, etc. From there we returned to Norfolk, where my host gave a banquet to two hundred and fifty people. Among the guests was ex-President Taft, who was then Professor of Law at Yale University. We sat next to each other at table and I had a lively conversation with the talkative and genial ex-President. He was well versed in conditions in Finland and showed lively interest in our constitutional and cultural struggle.

"Thereupon we started on the last of my journeys in America, at first two hundred miles by car through flowering districts and walnut woods to the city of Syracuse, followed by another day's journey in the same conveyance to Niagara. We stayed two days at the mighty falls. The wild and beautiful spectacle of the scenery gave me indescribable pleasure. I was told on this occasion that Americans and Englishmen pronounce it Niăgără (with the accent on the antepenultimate syllable and all the vowels short), while the Indians say, like ourselves, Niagāra. All musicians adopt the latter pronunciation.

"From Niagara we drove direct to New Haven, to the ceremony at Yale University.

"The conferring of degrees was a marvelous experience. The ceremony was marked by imposing ancient ceremonial. During the whole act my music was played. Over three thousand people were present. When the persons upon whom degrees were to be conferred, twenty-two in number, entered in procession, the orchestra played *Finlandia*. When all was over, *Spring Song* was played. The first to congratulate me after the ceremony was Taft."

The presentation of Sibelius for the degree of Doctor of Music was made to the president of the university, before an audience of several thousands, by Professor Wilbur L. Cross, later Governor of Connecticut, in the following words:

" By his music intensely national in inspiration and yet in sympathy with the mood of the West, Dr. Sibelius long since captured Finland, Germany, and England, and on coming to America to conduct a Symphonic Poem, found that his fame had already preceded him here also. Still in the prime of life, he has become, by the power and originality of his work, one of the most distinguished of living composers. What Wagner did with Teutonic legend, Dr. Sibelius has done in his own impressive way with the legends of Finland as embodied in her national epic. He has translated the Kalevala into the universal language of music, remarkable for its breadth, large simplicity, and the infusion of a deeply poetic personality."

The time for leaving America was approaching. Sibelius was not allowed to leave the soil of America before promising that he would return in the following year for a tour, with public performances in all the more important cities of the country. The World War, however, was destined to upset this program completely. Sibelius could have no presentiment of this in the hour of farewell and he looked forward with pleasure to paying another visit to the New World, which he, too, had learned to appreciate. In the relations between America and the Finnish composer mutual affection had been established.

"America was not only an entirely new country, it was also an entirely new climate. There was much there that impressed me as genuinely American, but at the same time much that was reminiscent of Europe. Above all, however, the atmosphere, the feeling in the air, was unique. Wealth meant a good deal, of course, but cultural interests were also pursued to a greater extent than was imagined at that time in Europe."

Sibelius spent the last days of his visit to America in New York. The city is notorious in the summer for its heat and humidity, which make life a torture to everyone, "so that you can imagine how I felt," says Sibelius.

It was with a sigh of relief that he went on board the *President Grant*, which was to carry him out to sea to the free world of blue expanses and fresh breezes.

While Sibelius was on board the liner, he and the other passengers heard the news of the murder in Sarajevo. The news was a great shock, though scarcely anyone could have foreseen the fateful consequences of the event.

On July 2 Sibelius reached Copenhagen, where he was met by his wife. In Copenhagen he was informed that a performance during the Baltic Exhibition in

Malmö had had to be canceled, because the authorities had not found it possible, out of consideration for Russia, to agree to his request that he should be described expressly as a Finnish composer in the program.

Sibelius was forced to realize the disadvantage of belonging to a small nation under the scepter of a great power — a handicap that played a bigger part in regard to the advancement of his art on foreign soil than I have attempted to describe. Some compensation was afforded him, however, by the news that at an exhibition of music arranged at that time by his publishers, Breitkopf & Härtel, in which a separate room was reserved for the world's most famous composers from Bach and Beethoven to Mendelssohn, Meyerbeer, Wagner, and Strauss, Breitkopf & Härtel had set aside a whole wall for Sibelius.

XXI

THE GREAT WAR

*Home once more — Whims and plans — The first
months of the war — Minor compositions — The fifth
symphony — Sibelius on the nature of symphonic
composition — Outbreak of the revolution.*

ON July 10 Sibelius landed in Åbo. Crowned with
fresh laurels and greater renown in a new world,
he nevertheless saw his own country again with joy.

"Finland is splendid," he exclaims immediately
after his return in a letter to an intimate friend. "What
a poetical and beautiful country we have! "

Sibelius revolved many plans in his head on his return from America. He meditated a symphonic poem,
King Fjalar. He had been approached by interested
parties on the subject of composing an opera founded
on Juhani Aho's *Juha*. He had been tempted by another proposal intended to provide him with considerably greater financial profit: a ballet, *Karhun Tap-
pajaiset (The Bear Hunters)*, after the *Kalevala*, which
it was proposed to stage in London.

Sibelius considered the schemes, but came to the conclusion that he could not accept them. He states his motives in a private letter:

" I cannot become a prolific writer. It would mean killing all my reputation and my art. I have made my name in the world by straightforward means. I must go on in the same way.

" Perhaps I am too much of a hypochondriac. But to waste on a few *pas* a motif that would be excellently suited to symphonic composition! "

Sibelius wishes to follow his own line. It is the idea of a new symphony that is in his mind. That plan, too, raises doubts which I will refer to later on.

Then the World War broke out.

" The outbreak of the war was a complete surprise to me," Sibelius admits. " I had never seriously imagined that the largest nations in Europe would start a war with each other. In spite of all we had read in the papers during the last few years about international relations being strained, I had the conviction that the Franco-Prussian War was the last armed conflict between civilized nations in Europe.

" It was generally thought at first, as I did, that the war would not last more than three months. It was therefore impossible at first to take it as tragically as the situation demanded — it would have been another matter if one could have imagined in advance what years of indescribable misery it was to cause.

" When it appeared subsequently that the war was going to be a prolonged one, the situation grew serious for me personally owing to communications being interrupted with my German publishers, whose fees were my principal source of income, as at that time and for a long time afterwards Finland was not a party to the Bern Convention, so that I was deprived of the income I might have had from the performances of my works abroad. The strange attitude of our country towards the Bern Convention kept me for a long time in an extremely unfavorable financial position in comparison to my colleagues on the Continent. I did not derive the slightest material benefit from the fact that my works were played to a growing extent in the musical centers throughout the world. It is only during the last few years that there has been a change in these abnormal conditions.

" The connection with Breitkopf & Härtel was, however, arranged through Wilhelm Hansen, of Copenhagen, who also published much of my work himself. I also soon found an English publisher."

During the early part of the war Sibelius sought oblivion from the turmoil around him in composing diligently. The visible traces of this work are represented by a number of minor pieces, mostly for the piano.

" In looking through the notes in my diary during the first months of the war I see that from August to the middle of November I wrote sixteen minor compositions."

The composing of these pieces on a small scale was a narcotic. They must not make us think that Sibelius did not feel profoundly the events that convulsed the world. He was intensely moved by what he witnessed.

" How much pathos there is in our time! " he says in a letter written at the end of the first months of the war. " We are approaching the foreseen religious era. But it is impossible to define a religion — least of all in words. But perhaps music is a mirror."

The Sibelius whose reactions to the events of the time we can witness is expressed in the fifth symphony, the ideas and moods of which were constantly revolving in his brain. The clarity he aims at is not easy to gain at a time of general chaos. But his intuition guides him along the right path and allows him to perceive what he surmises even in hours of despondency and doubt.

" In a deep dell again. But I already begin to see dimly the mountain that I shall certainly ascend. . . . God opens His door for a moment and His orchestra plays the fifth symphony."

This note is from the end of September 1914; it shows that then already the ideas for the fifth symphony had begun to shape themselves in Sibelius's mind.

As already mentioned, Sibelius proceeded in great hesitation along the road he had taken.

" I was uncertain whether I should begin on the fifth symphony. I have, indeed, had to suffer a good deal for having persevered in composing symphonies at a time when practically all composers turned to other forms of expression. My stubbornness was an eyesore to many critics and conductors and it is really only in recent years that opinion has begun to change. Perhaps the name injured my symphonies, but once they represent what I understand under the idea of a symphony I could not very well provide them with labels that would give a wrong impression of what I aimed at. The current idea had to be extended.

" I do not wish to give a reasoned exposition of the essence of symphony. I have expressed my opinion in my works. I should like, however, to emphasize a point that I consider essential: the directly symphonic is the compelling vein that goes through the whole. This in contrast to the depicting."

A year later the fifth symphony in E flat major came to completion — that monumental work in which the master's creative spirit soared like an eagle in the sun above a tortured and broken world. The symphony

234

proved an expression of its author's strong optimism, gained through suffering, in an evil time an uplifting testimony to an indomitable faith in life's ever renovating power, to a manly attitude towards existence, which Sibelius expressed at about the same time in the sentence:

" This life that I love so infinitely, a feeling that must stamp everything I compose."

During the first year of the war Sibelius had not been able to devote his powers solely to the fifth symphony. Worries regarding his livelihood, essential even for an artist, had obliged him to engage in minor compositions for the piano and for violin with piano accompaniment. Among these we find such pearls as *Pensées Lyriques*, opus 40, for piano and the sonata in E major for violin and piano, which was completed on March 12, 1915. Among the minor compositions in 1915, however, many would, perhaps, be inclined to award the palm to the five glorious songs for male chorus to words by Fröding and Reuter, combined in opus 84.

The work on the fifth symphony had in addition been interrupted by tours in Scandinavia with concerts in Stockholm, Göteborg, Oslo, and Bergen. These tours were repeated during the spring of 1916.

The fifth symphony was performed for the first time

in public at a concert Sibelius gave on his fiftieth birthday. At this concert the *Oceanides* and two violin serenades of 1912–13 were also played.

Sibelius's fiftieth birthday was celebrated as a national holiday. The ovations began early in the morning, when the master arrived at the practice rooms of the Helsingfors Municipal Orchestra to conduct a rehearsal of that evening's concert. They continued throughout the day in the form of deputations and callers and reached their height at an evening reception, when the leading men of Finland in various spheres of activity combined in honoring the composer as Finland's greatest son. Among the speakers was Professor Werner Söderhjelm, who extolled the friend of his youth in a speech marked by great feeling and inspired rhetoric. I quote some parts of this speech that afford an excellent illustration of the position Sibelius had attained as a leading national and cultural figure:

" The man whom we honor today is still — he has just given us splendid proof of it — in the height of summer in his production, and yet he has a life's work behind him of such extent and importance that on this day, when he has not got beyond the limit of the first half-century, the whole of his country feels the necessity of offering him its gratitude and assuring him of its admiration and love. It is said that we are a musical nation. Perhaps we really have a sounding-board in our disposition that vibrates more sensitively to the art of sounds than any other, excepting of words. But to how few of us it is really granted to force our way into the high and enclosed world in which Mistress Musica is enthroned, to understand fully the secrets in her supernatural language and to devote ourselves to her worship with the rapture of all our senses! How many of us really know what it is that makes Jean Sibelius stand so great, so unique and lonely in the annals of modern music, makes him a renovator of forms, makes him blend realism and romanticism like all great artists in reality, frank feelings and a strong sense of reality with the flight of imagination and the mysticism of poetry? Yet more than one of his works has grown into the consciousness of us all and become national poetry, and for more than one of us laymen, who listened unreflectingly to his music, something of these works has become a mirror of what we ourselves experienced in our innermost hearts in feelings and struggles, in the uplifting of the mind and the sorrowing of the heart. And what at any rate we all understand is that in Sibelius we possess one of the richest spirits that were ever born in this country and the greatest creative power now living among us. We also know that the geniuses that a small country has fostered shine like never dying torches over its footsteps in the history of civilization, eternally preserving them from being effaced. There is no power or time that can destroy what a nation has created in great spiritual works. However near destruc-

tion it may be brought, in them it will always find a
fresh call to valor in its struggle against fate. Yes, if it be
its fate to be destroyed, it will survive itself in what it has
produced through its best spirits and one day it will
celebrate its resurrection through them. We know all
this and feel it all the more at a time when the whole
world around us is shaken to its foundations. Is it surprising, then, that we should direct our warmest thoughts of
gratitude to a man who has given us such inalienable
wealth?

" A great artist, who creates out of the consciousness of
his people, is like the giant tree of the fairy-tale, whose
roots penetrate to the innermost parts of the earth and
whose crown touches the fastness of the heavens. But
an art such as Sibelius's has its roots not only in the earth
we walk on and from which we have all grown. They
reach deep down to regions where the mold ends and fire
dwells, where the most hidden powers live and the treasures of the nation's soul are purified, to be brought forth
to the light of day only once in a century by a divinely
gifted genius. . . .

" Nothing is more difficult to define than the ' national trait' in such an extraordinarily varied spirit as
Sibelius, and there is nothing more dangerous than to
trace his essential qualities back to anything so indefinite.
However strong and striking may be the Finnish under-
tone that gives so many of his compositions their special
character, however much of our fate we find interpreted
in them, it is always the personality itself that gives the

238

work its greatest originality and sets the stamp of genius
on it. It is scarcely possible to speak of tendencies in work
that moves forward with the breadth and restlessness of
beating waves, but perhaps we catch glimpses of endeavors, growing more definite in the course of time, towards the development of this purely personal feature
and away from all that, even in the widest sense, can be
called schedule. I am merely thinking of a comparison
between the *Kullervo* symphony and the later symphonies
or between the other mythological tone-poems and the
composition that, to me at any rate, is the most moving
revelation of the artist's innermost soul and is even entitled accordingly, *Voces Intimæ*, the string quartet. But
with this intensified subjectivity Sibelius's art does not
lose any of its special features nor of its wealth. Constantly fresh sources seem to open up, from which it
only has to gush forth: they spout upward from his personality's store of images of thought and fantasy that
seems to be inexhaustible. And we follow this line of
development ourselves in our relationship to Sibelius:
if we were formerly attracted to him by the perception
that his music combined and made outwardly visible what
was to us a valuable spiritual national possession, we
have now learned to admire and love him because he is
just himself, Jean Sibelius, and because his music expresses just what he feels and thinks.

"The significance of a national contribution to universal art consists in this, that the existing sphere of
material or forms is widened by new, specific values, char-

239

acteristic of the spirit of a certain nation. But in order that these should gain their full value and be appropriated by all, the artist must with the power of genius be able to force all to listen to him. No art rules over such wide landmarks as those of music, but neither is any art, perhaps, so bound by rules once fixed. More evenly than that of many another new and independently thinking musical composer, Sibelius's path has been through the musical world a triumphal progress, it might be said, in which jealousy and slanderers, who are never lacking in the footsteps of genius, were soon brought to silence. His originality has not stood in the light of his high culture, his personality in the light of his profoundly human qualities, his intelligence in the light of his heart. Thus he has provided the spiritual culture of our time with the greatest contribution that has so far been given it from a Finnish source and has taken his place as the representative of his people among the noblest in art."

Jean Sibelius had already for a dozen years taken a different road from that on which he had gained the victories of his early manhood and his unique popularity. In the effort to realize his most intimate and innermost self he had often experienced the thorns and thistles of an artist's career, had learned the unavoidable loneliness of creative genius. The nation's spontaneous ovation on his fiftieth birthday afforded him lively evidence that in the greatness and bright calm of his maturity he possessed the love, gratitude, and admiration of his people beyond anyone in his own country.

The master in the far north was still cut off from the world, where his music had already begun its conquest, as long as the war carried on its work of destruction. The concert tours in Scandinavia were his only connecting link with the world beyond the frontiers of Finland. They afforded him an opportunity of escaping for a time from the oppression that rested on his country, but did not enable him to renew contact with the great world, in which, after a hard struggle, he had at last begun to make his presence felt.

No wonder that Sibelius's mind was sometimes filled with gloom, while the shadows of war descended more thickly over the earth. In his notes and letters we find outbursts such as these lines written in the autumn of 1916:

"I often ask myself: Is my life to pass in complete isolation from the great civilized countries? Am I no more to experience the delight that a first-class orchestra gives me when I conduct my works?

"But perhaps I look at things too gloomily."

Just as frequently, however, his philosophical vein, his uplift over the adversities of the moment, assert themselves.

"One should really study astronomy daily. This

in order always to be able to place our friend Tellus correctly. In its modest little place in the universe, I mean."

During 1916 a number of compositions appeared, in which the master created works of enchanting beauty in a small framework. We need only mention the six songs, opus 86, to words by Tavaststjerna, Karlfeldt, Snoilsky, and Lybeck and the music for Hofmannsthal's *Jedermann*, in which, in the midst of the horrors of a modern war, Sibelius succeeded in conjuring forth illusory medieval moods of unworldly mysticism — truly an imposing proof of strength of mind. When the music for Hofmannsthal's mystery play had been completed, in the beginning of October 1916, Sibelius proceeded to revise the fifth symphony, with a view to still greater concentration in contents and form. The revised version was publicly performed at a symphonic concert on December 14, 1916, when the fifth symphony was played in what its author then thought was its "final form." In this Sibelius underestimated the severity of his self-criticism, which grew more and more merciless as time went on; the symphony did not obtain its final form until three years later.

The third winter of the war set in without the strife between the nations showing any signs of abating.

On the other hand it brought about a change that affected Finland very closely. Russian Tsardom perished; its enormous military power was shaken by a flood of anarchy, the most terrifying manifestations of which Helsingfors was forced to witness.

" The Russian revolution," says Sibelius, " made itself felt even in our peaceful Järvenpää. Since the beginning of the war the district had harbored a strong military force. Now the men began to settle accounts with their officers. The murder of officers was a daily occurrence here, as in Helsingfors and other large military centers. Shots were heard all day long. The growing arrogance and savagery of the working classes made things look bad for us, too. Workmen's riots, unrest, and strikes during the summer, which even the Järvenpää district was not spared, gave us a foretaste of what was in store. A horrible time."

Sibelius's faith in humanity was subjected to a severe test. Though once upon a time the creator of *Kullervo*, he had in his mature manhood acquired a well-balanced Apollonian view of life that did not even allow him to find æsthetic satisfaction in the eruption of primitive passions that poured forth from the depths of the sea of people. Impotent against the reality that men had created, he tried, as so often before, to find strength in untouched nature.

" As I turn the pages of my diary of those days,

243

I find that I did my best to forget the evil of the times in studying nature around me.

" On April 18, 1917 I wrote:

" ' There are twelve swans on the lake. I saw them through my field-glasses. I also saw six wild geese and an eagle. Strangely poetical, unique.'

" A few days later:

" ' A wonderful day, spring and life. The earth smells, mutes and fortissimo. An extraordinary light, reminiscent of a haze in August.' "

Intimate contact with nature enabled him to devote himself with undiminished power to producing fresh beauties. The twelve songs to words by Runeberg and Franzén, mostly written during the spring of 1917, form imperishable proof of the healthy unaffectedness of his inspiration. During the summer some works of larger size were conceived: five Humoresques for violin and orchestra. " Life's sorrow and rays of sunshine " — thus Sibelius characterizes them in a private letter, and continues: " I like them very much. They are ' large size.' "

As the summer was drawing to an end, Sibelius found strength in him for a new symphony in spite of the turmoil around him. At the same time he decided to subject the fifth symphony to a new and final revision, from which the work was to emerge in hardened and tempered firmness.

XXII

IN THE POWER OF
THE REDS

*Civil war breaks out — The doings of the Reds in
Järvenpää — A house search — Sibelius succeeds in
moving to Helsingfors — The approach of the Germans — The relief of Helsingfors.*

VENTS followed each other with astounding ra-
pidity. The November strike with its bloody
atrocities gave appalling proof of the primitive instincts
that had taken possession of the minds of the Finnish
working classes. December brought the acknowledg-
ment of Finland's independence, but with some tens
of thousands of demoralized Russian troops fraterniz-
ing with Finnish Reds and a strong Bolshevik fleet outside the capital, independence was not worth much.
The elements in favor of preserving social order did
not lose heart. They prepared for battle. On January
28, 1918 civil war broke out.

245

Possessed of an indomitable strength of will, Sibelius had by this time got as far as the third movement of his new symphony. It is scarcely necessary to say that the doings of the Reds, as savage in Järvenpää as in other places, where they could give free rein to their instincts, interfered with his creative ability. The new aspect of the revolution roused Sibelius both as a patriot and as an artist.

" The Reds behave like wild beasts," says an entry in his diary on one of the first days of the revolt. " All educated people are in danger of their lives. Murder upon murder. Soon, no doubt, my hour will come, for I must be specially hateful to them as the composer of patriotic music."

At the beginning of February Sibelius was informed by the local staff in Järvenpää that he was forbidden to leave the precincts of his villa. Whether the prohibition was dictated by a wish to annoy or with a view to his safety, it is impossible to say. In any case the news made him conscious of how precarious his position was in a district that was entirely in the power of the Reds.

He did his utmost, however, to distract his attention from the situation, as he could do nothing to alter it. He endeavored to forget everything by working on his symphony. The prohibition from the staff is entered in his diary in a few words, followed by a despair-

JEAN SIBELIUS

ing exclamation: " But what has all this to do with my symphony? If only I could get away from it all! "

This was, however, no easy matter. A few days after the first warning he received a new one — a threatening confirmation of how dangerous his position really was. Sibelius relates this as follows:

" On February 11 a detachment of Red Guards came to search my house. They were looking for hidden supplies of food and arms. The men presented a terrifying appearance with their pock-marked, deformed faces. They were not from the Järvenpää district — a circumstance that made my position all the more dangerous. They had no idea of who I was and behaved in a very threatening and rough manner. I actually had a revolver hidden in a room on the ground floor of the villa. The house-porter, who was present during the search, knew of this, and if he had betrayed me my life would not have been worth much."

The servant's loyalty stood the test, however. There must have been some human feelings about these Red Guards, for, when Sibelius seated himself at the piano at one part of the search in order to calm his terrified children, one of the men who had been placed on guard in the kitchen said to the maid:

" It must be very pleasant for you to serve in a house where you hear such lovely music."

Two days later, on February 13, Sibelius's villa was

searched again, this time by a crowd of Red Guards who behaved in an even wilder manner than the first. Sibelius's entry in his diary displays a raging fury. But it is not the supporter of social order who is incensed by the insolence of the champions of the lower classes, but the aristocrat, the individualist, the artist, who reacts with every fiber of his being to the brutal invasion of the sanctity of his private life.

"We have again had Red Guards searching the house. What a shame for my house that I had to allow them to open all drawers and saw the 'treasures' of this poor, destitute house exposed! When I saw this, I could scarcely restrain my grief. A crowd of bandits, armed to the teeth, and I, a nervous composer, unarmed! They say that one should give way to violence. This one can do, but it is more difficult to bear dishonor that has been suffered by one's house. What a life!"

During the succeeding days the isolated home in Järvenpää heard news of fresh murders, among them of many people who had been intimate with Sibelius in their lifetime. The diary affords evidence of further heroic efforts to continue working, but it also tells of times at which this was quite impossible.

On February 17 Sibelius heard that his brother Christian, senior doctor at the Lappviken Central Asylum, had been imprisoned by the Reds, but had been released. Christian Sibelius had been instructed by the staff in Helsingfors to have places ready for Red Guards who had lost their reason during battles at the front. Firmly determined to carry out this order only in the last extremity, Professor Sibelius had replied that his asylum was absolutely full at the moment, but, being excitable and outspoken, he could not resist sneering at the Red authorities by saying: " Besides, the whole lot of you are mad." This outspokenness incurred the displeasure of the Reds and might easily have cost him dear.

Bravely endeavoring to bury himself in himself and his work of composing, Jean Sibelius would not, in spite of the warnings he had been given and in spite of the example of the fate of many of his friends, seriously admit how dangerous it was for him to remain in the country surrounded by Reds who did not know him and could consequently not be supposed to be willing to pay the slightest attention either to his age or to his special position as the greatest artist in Finland. His friends in Helsingfors had repeatedly tried to induce him to move into the town, where it was in any case safer, but their arguments had not been successful. The matter was finally brought to a head at a meeting between his brother Christian, his brother-in-law Eero Järnefelt, and Robert Kajanus, when it was decided to send Kajanus as an envoy to Järvenpää. One day early in March Kajanus, escorted by two Red Guards, ar-

rived at Sibelius's villa, spoke seriously with the unworldly master, urged the responsibility he had to his
country and himself, and finally induced him to move
with his family to Helsingfors.

Sibelius and his family put up at his brother's at the
Lappviken Asylum and waited for the end of the War
of Liberation. Bodily privations were added to the
suspense as to the outcome of the struggle. The sojourn at Lappviken was a regular starvation cure. Strict
rationing had been introduced in the capital in general,
but the Whites at the Lappviken Asylum had a particularly bad time. The explanation was simple.

" My brother had at last, in spite of his protests, been
forced to accept Red patients, masses of whom were
sent there. The servants of the asylum consisted
chiefly of Reds, so that they did not recognize any
duties towards us, but in distributing food supplies
gave the preference to men of their own party and
themselves, so that the gentry received much less than
they were entitled to. As a result I lost forty pounds
in weight during the weeks we lived at the Lappviken
Asylum. The photograph of me that was taken after
the thinning cure certainly provides eloquent proof."

The days passed in suspense that increased as the
hope of release grew stronger. When the news was received of the rapid advance of the German troops, the

result could no longer be a matter of doubt as far as the capital was concerned, but none could tell what fate might befall any of its inhabitants in the turmoil of the final struggle.

On Thursday, April 11, the sound of guns could be heard at Alberga. It gave Sibelius an artistic sensation that surpassed almost everything he had experienced before. His diary says:

"April 11 during the bombardment. Have never dreamed of anything so tremendous. Horrible, but grand! Shall I be alive tomorrow?"

"The crescendo, as the thunder of the guns came nearer," Sibelius says later, "a crescendo that lasted for close on thirty hours and ended in a fortissimo I could never have dreamed of, was really a great sensation."

Fortunately, his apprehensions for the next day were unfounded. The relief of Helsingfors was accomplished with such slight sacrifice of blood and human lives as no one had dared to hope for, least of all those who had imagined that the Reds would at the last moment take a desperate revenge for their shattered hopes by a bloody massacre. In the afternoon of April 12 the first German troops entered Helsingfors and on the following morning the capital was entirely released. Soon the whole of South Finland was able to breathe freely again. Now at length the spring had come — a spring of reawakened courage for the people of Finland, of great patriotic transports and joyful trust in the future.

A painful stage of Sibelius's life had ended — a stage that he cannot look back upon to the present day without bitterness and sadness.

XXIII

ON THE HEIGHTS

Creative power — Three symphonies planned — Concert tours — Last meeting with Busoni — Sibelius's sixtieth birthday — A world-wide celebrity — The guiding line in Sibelius's life — Sibelius on contemporary music — Conclusion.

WONDERFULLY intense mood sways Sibelius at the end of the prolonged nerve-racking period beginning with the World War and ending in the Finnish civil war. A vein of tragedy runs in the depth of this mood, but a broad feeling of creative power predominates. He had worked incessantly during the whole turbulent time following the Russian revolution; he was not idle even during his enforced isolation in the spring of 1918, when, during the general suspense and uncertainty, he composed a big work for chorus and orchestra, *Oma maa*, which he himself describes as " a song of praise to the scenery and light nights of Finland " — in the capital of the Red Terror! And yet

253

when he comes forth again into life and among people, it seems as if he were beset by a single thought — to make good the omissions of a long period of idleness by means of hard work, while the world around him is given over to a festive intoxication of joy after all the trials it had suffered.

Ideas simply seethe in his brain. He struggles bravely once more to turn the fifth symphony into the ideal work he had seen in the far-seeing vision of his genius; simultaneously the sixth symphony and the plans for the seventh mature within him.

Sibelius himself describes his mood in a wonderful comparison in a private letter of May 20, 1918:

". . . as if I were preparing to quit this life and in descending into my grave shot an eagle on the wing — sighted well and skillfully without a thought of what was in store."

In the same extraordinary letter he describes his scheme of work:

" *My new works — partly sketched and planned.*

" The Vth symphony in a new form — practically composed anew — I work at daily. Movement I entirely new, movement II reminiscent of the old, movement III reminiscent of the end of the I movement of the old. Movement IV the old motifs, but stronger in revision. The whole, if I may say so, a vital climax to the end. Triumphal.

"The VIth symphony is wild and impassioned in character. Somber, with pastoral contrasts. Probably in 4 movements, with the end rising to a somber roaring of the orchestra, in which the main theme is drowned.

Facsimile of an extract from Sibelius's letter dated
May 20, 1918

"The VIIth symphony. Joy of life and vitality, with appassionato passages. In 3 movements — the last a ' Hellenic rondo.'

"All this with due reservation. . . . It looks as if I was to come out with all these three symphonies at the same time.

" As usual, the sculptural more prominent in my music. Hence this hammering on the ethical line that takes hold of me entirely and on which I must concentrate and hold out. . . .

" With regard to symphonies VI and VII the plans may possibly be altered according to the development of the musical ideas. As usual, I am a slave to my themes and submit to their demands.

" By all this I see how my innermost self has changed since the days of the IVth symphony. And these symphonies of mine are more in the nature of professions of faith than my other works."

As impatient as a young composer who is consumed with longing to strike his great blow, the fifty-two-year-old master sets out to resume the battle with his genius, while the world is preparing to get back into normal ways. The program sketched above is carried out, though on slightly different lines.

" The reservation in my statement about the two new symphonies," says Sibelius, " was fully justified. The fifth symphony was not completed in its final form until the autumn of 1919 and a long time was to elapse before its two successors appeared, and then not exactly in the form I had originally intended. The final form of one's work is, indeed, dependent on powers that are stronger than oneself. Later on, one can sub-

256

stantiate this or that, but on the whole one is merely a tool. This wonderful logic — let us call it God — that governs a work of art is the forcing power."

While the symphonies were maturing, Sibelius developed a truly astounding productivity in other spheres: two big cantatas for chorus and orchestra — *Jordens Sång*, to words by Jarl Hemmer, and *Maan Virsi*, to words by Eino Leino — minor pieces for piano, and tone-poems in a concentrated form for orchestra.

Sibelius also found time for concert tours abroad.

"In January 1921," he says, "I was engaged for a concert in Queen's Hall in London with Busoni, who on that occasion played his *Indian Fantasy*, while I performed the fourth symphony. During the whole of the war Busoni had been an assiduous champion of my music, which he played in Germany and Switzerland. I could not imagine that it was to be the last time that I saw my faithful old friend. He seemed so full of vitality and so buoyant.

"At New Year's 1923, I was engaged for concerts in Norway and Sweden. When I started on January 14 — I have the date from the notes in my diary — three sections of the seventh symphony were ready. On my return home the whole symphony was completed; I performed it in public at a concert in Helsingfors on

257

February 19 — the last time that I conducted in Finland. Then I went to Rome, where I conducted a concert in the Augusteo on March 11.

"On March 2, 1924, at night, as I entered in my diary, I completed 'Fantasia Sinfonica' — that was what I at first thought of calling my seventh symphony in one movement."

In 1925 we find Sibelius struggling with a gigantic task: composing the music for Shakspere's *The Tempest* in execution of an order from Det Kongelige Theater in Copenhagen. At the same time he wrestles with two *Kalevala* subjects, *Tapiola* and *Väinö's Song*, from which a symphonic poem and a tone-poem for chorus and orchestra emerged.

In the midst of this hard work the master was overtaken by his sixtieth birthday. The ovations on his fiftieth birthday are repeated, but the dominant note is different. In 1915 it was an oppressed nation that demonstratively honored the man to whom it was granted to proclaim its love of liberty with greater power and weight than anyone else. Now it is a free country that requites its greatest son. The head of the State awards him the highest order of the republic, the representatives of the people resolve, without a division, to award him the largest State pension that had ever been granted to a private Finnish citizen, society

258

JEAN SIBELIUS
by N. Koussevitzky, 1935

again exerts its utmost powers to declare the undiminished intensity of its feelings.

It is a man of world-wide fame who is honored this time by a small country in the far north. Sibelius's music has completed its triumphal progress and now the composer can point to outwardly visible proofs of his fame. The fall of the Tsarist power and the liberation of Finland have removed the last obstacle for foreign countries, too, to honor Sibelius officially as one of the pillars of the building that suffers such heavy affliction at present under the name of Western culture. One great honor after another has been showered upon him, the mighty ones of the world have singled him out, and the most distinguished societies in his own profession have competed to be able to number him among their elect.

Sibelius has recently entered upon his eighth decade, and the development during his jubilee year has only provided fresh confirmatory evidence of the undiminished vitality of his noble art.

World-wide recognition must, of course, have pleased a man who, almost half a century ago, appeared rather a suspicious person, when as a descendant of a conservative class of society he chose the singular career of a musician. Sibelius was able with greater ease of conscience to garner the outward evidence of his

victories, seeing that he was conscious of having created his masterpieces without ever giving heed to other
voices than that of his own artistic conscience.

But outward success and all the prospects it opened
up in various directions have not deflected the guiding
lines of Sibelius's life. He has received many offers to
transfer his activities to more pretentious external conditions — for instance, in 1920, when he was invited
to undertake the leadership of the celebrated Eastman
School of Music at the University of Rochester. But
he prefers to remain in the surroundings that have provided the most fruitful conditions for his creative work.

Here, in his beloved Järvenpää, he leads a kind of
double existence, as before. While the name of Sibelius decorates the concert programs in the musical capitals of the world and tempts the greatest exponents of
the present day, the celebrated bearer of that name remains quietly in the countryside of Nyland, continuing
his work. " Now that my youth is past, my work and
whole development are on a different plane. Formerly
I longed to go out into the world, and I have, indeed,
lived a good deal in the great world abroad. Now it is
the quietude up here that is dearest to me." Creative
work is the mature master's passion as it was the passion of the enthusiastic youth. Sibelius testifies to this
himself:

" Composing has been the guiding line in my life,
260

and it still is so. My work has the same fascination for me as when I was young, a fascination bound up with the difficulty of the task. Let no one imagine that composing is easier for an old composer if he takes his art seriously. The demands one makes on oneself have increased in the course of years. Greater sureness makes one scorn solutions that come too easily, that follow the line of least resistance, in a higher degree than formerly. One is always faced with new problems. The thing that has pleased me most is that I have been able to reject. The greatest labor I have expended, perhaps, was on works that have never been completed."

Sibelius is still governed today by the feeling of creative yearning and overflowing creative power that held him enthralled at the time the Finnish War of Liberation came to an end. Nevertheless, the tragic-pathetic has been displaced by inspiring powers of a brighter hue. The eighteen years that have passed since 1918 have provided him with the answer to many questions, dispelled many doubts and led his unremittingly searching spirit to greater clearness about himself. His inspiration still plays on a many-toned register: the lyricism in the sixth symphony, the power of imagination in *Tapiola*, the dramatic intensity in the music to *The Tempest* combine to make of the latest phase of his creative work a fascinating synthesis of all his production. But the predominating feature is the Apollonian joy in light, clarity, strength, and chaste form that can already be seen clearly in the second symphony, that entirely governs the third and is temporarily obscured during the years of doubtful musing, of uncompromisingly severe self-examination, of which Voces Intimæ and the fourth symphony stand as an impressive monument, to be victoriously affirmed in the radiant apotheosis of the fifth symphony; this Apollonian worship of light sheds its golden glory over Sibelius's seventh symphony. The romantic and the naturalist still live in the ever youthful master, but the clearness, self-command, and grand style of the classic control them both.

From the pinnacles of intellectual maturity and artistic perfection Sibelius looks down with generous sympathy for all humanity on the life and phenomena around him, particularly on phenomena in his own sphere of activity.

" When you have lived as long as I," he says, " and have seen one tendency after another being born, blossom, and die, you are inclined to take up a less decided position. You prefer to search for what is good, wherever you can find it. In doing so you often discover that almost every musical ' school,' even if it has on the whole aimed at a goal that you cannot approve, has, nevertheless, in some respect or other had something good about it. The surprising thing is that even those periods that have yielded the least direct gain have certainly had their own great importance. Even mistakes exist in order to widen the horizon, and, for instance, with regard to the atonic music of twenty years ago, even that has left something good behind it, at any rate in a technical sense. In this connection I must confess that if I were young again, but equipped with the experience life has given me, I think that I should therefore be considerably more appreciative of Wagner than I once was. My decided antagonism to Wagner in my youth was, I fancy, dictated to some extent by the fear of being subjected to an influence that I had seen taking possession of so many of my friends, both old and young. And yet I still place Verdi higher than Wagner. Opera is, after all, a conventional form of art and should be cultivated as such.

"The composer for me above all others is Beethoven. I am affected as powerfully by the human side of him as by his music. He is a revelation to me. He was a Titan. Everything was against him and yet he triumphed."

Sibelius's views on contemporary composers are characterized by understanding, although his critical acumen will not be denied.

"If you look at it thoroughly, I believe that there is a kind of freemasonry among composers owing to things having been and being so difficult for us. All of us have to reckon with the critics and the public.

For my part, thanks to the experience of a long lifetime, I have learned to accept disappointment and reverses with resignation. Scarcely one of my best works was met with the right understanding when first performed. They took at least twenty years to succeed. With regard to immediate success I have long since been cured of all illusions.

" I find much that is interesting in present-day music, although I cannot be in sympathy with all the tendencies that have been expressed within the last few decades. There has been too much experimenting, and unaffected feeling has not always been allowed to come into its own.

" The error of our day has long been its faith in polyphony. It has seemed as if people imagined that the whole had become better by placing nonentities on top of each other. Polyphony is, of course, a force when there is good reason for it, but for a long time it has almost seemed as if an illness had been raging among composers.

" The instrumentation in many modern works has been too showy — ' fire in your mouth to scare the children.'

" I have not been able to avoid the impression, too, that much, yes, too much, in present-day music has very little connection with life. The themes often seem artificial, the elaboration mechanical.

264

"At one time it appeared to me that many present-day composers lacked what the great Swedish poet Rydberg called joy in life. They made one think of court councilors composing, their works made one think of doctors' dissertations.

"That was then. Now that these gods have been cast down I feel optimistic."

Joy in life, care-free indifference to the opinions and moods of the day, freedom from sordid calculation, fascinated reverence for the mystery of art, fearlessness, honesty — in all this the honored master is still associated with the youth who once upon a time set out boldly towards an unknown future. The noble structure of his works has come forth from the grand line of his life. He has won his inner strength and harmony in a hard battle. In a disjointed time, a period of dissension, Jean Sibelius provides us with the uplifting picture of a man who dared to follow his genius and never was subservient to other claims than those of his own artistic conscience, who dared to live his life in the grand style.

LIST OF

JEAN SIBELIUS'S WORKS

JEAN SIBELIUS'S

WORKS

ABBREVIATIONS OF PUBLISHERS' NAMES:

A. H.   = Abr. Hirsch (Stockholm).
Au.   = Augener (London).
B. & H. = Breitkopf & Härtel (Leipzig).
C.   = Chappel (London).
F.   = Fischer (New York).
F-r.   = Fazer (Helsingfors).
H.   = Hansen (Copenhagen).
H-m.   = Holm (Helsingfors).
S.   = Schlesinger (Berlin).
U.   = Universal (Vienna).
W.   = Westerlund (Helsingfors).

The majority of the works published by Breitkopf & Härtel and by Hansen have also been published in Finland by Fazer or Westerlund.

A. With opus numbers

Opus	Title	Date	Place	Publisher
1.	Five Christmas Songs	1895	Helsingfors	W.
2.	Two pieces for violin: Romance ⎱ revised Epilogue ⎰ in 1912	1888	Lovisa	U.

Opus Title	Date	Place	Publisher
3. Arioso (Runeberg), for voice and string orchestra, revised in 1911 .	1893	Helsingfors	W.
4. String Quartet in B flat major	1889	Lovisa	Ms.
5. Six Impromptus for piano	1893	Helsingfors	B. & H.
6. Cassation, for small orchestra	1895	Helsingfors	Ms.
7. Kullervo, symphonic poem for orchestra, soli, and chorus	1892	Lovisa-H:fors	Ms.
8. Incidental music to Odlan (Lybeck), for orchestra . . .	1909	Järvenpää	Ms.
9. En Saga, tone-poem for orchestra, revised in 1901 . .	1892	Helsingfors	B. & H.
10. Karelia, overture for orchestra	1893	Ruovesi	B. & H.
11. Karelia, suite for orchestra . . . . Intermezzo Ballade Alla Marcia	1893	Ruovesi	B. & H.
12. Sonata in F major for piano	1893	Ruovesi	B. & H.

Opus	Title	Date	Place	Publisher
13. Seven songs of Runeberg:				Otava.
'Neath the Fir Trees ⎫				
The Hope of the ⎬		1892	Pielisjärvi	
Kiss .... ⎭				
The Heart's Morning .... ⎫				
Spring is Flying ... ⎬		1891	Vienna	
The Dream ...... ⎭				
To Frigga		1892	Pielisjärvi	
The Young Sportsman		1891	Vikan	
14. Rakastava (The Lover), suite for string orchestra..		1911	H:fors-Paris	W.
15. Skogsrået (Rydberg), recitation to the accompaniment of piano, two horns, and string orchestra		1894	Helsingfors	Ms.
16. Spring Song, for orchestra		1894	Helsingfors	B. & H.
17. Seven songs with piano accompaniment:				B. & H.
And I questioned then no further (Runeberg)		1899	Kervo	
Slumber ⎫				
Enticement ⎬ (Tavaststjerna)		1894		
Astray ⎭				

Opus	Title	Date	Place	Publisher
17. Seven songs with piano accompaniment — *continued.*				
The Dragon-fly (Levertin)				
To Evening (Forsman)	1898	Kervo		
Driftwood (Calamnius)	1898	Lojo		
18. Six part-songs for male voices *a cappella:*			B. & H.
Sortunut ääni (Kanteletar)				
Terve kuu (Kalevala)	1901	Kervo		
Venematka (Kalevala)	1893	Helsingfors		
Saarella palaa (Kanteletar)				
Metsämiehen laulu Sydämeni laulu (Kivi)	1895	Waania		
19. Impromptu for female chorus and orchestra, revised in 1910	1902	Helsingfors	B. & H.
20. *Malinconia,* for 'cello and piano	1901	Kervo		

272

Opus	Title	Date	Place	Publisher
21.	Natus in curas, hymn for male voices a cappella			B. & H.
22.	Four *Legends* for orchestra:			
	Lemminkäinen and the Maidens ... Lemminkäinen in Tuonela	1895	Helsingfors	Ms.
	The Swan of Tuonela	1893	Kuopio	B. & H.
	The Return of Lemminkäinen	1895	Waania	B. & H.
23.	Cantata for the year 1897, for mixed chorus a cappella	1897	Helsingfors	B. & H.
24.	Ten Pieces for piano:			
	Impromptu ...... Romance in A flat	1894	Waania	
	Caprice .... Romance .... Waltz .... Idyll .... Andantino	1895	Helsingfors	
	Nocturne	1900	Berlin	
	Romance in D flat Barcarolle	1903	Helsingfors	
25.	Scènes historiques, I: All' Overtura Scène Festivo, revised 1911	1899	Helsingfors	B. & H.

Opus	Title	Date	Place	Publisher
26.	*Finlandia,* tone-poem for orchestra, revised in 1900	1899	Helsingfors	B. & H.
27.	Incidental music to *King Christian II* (Adolf Paul):			B. & H.
	Elégie .... Musette .... Minuet .... Fool's Song	1898	Helsingfors	
	Nocturne .... Serenade .... Ballade	1898	Lojo	
28.	*Sandels* (Runeberg), improvisation for male voices and orchestra	1898	Berlin	Ms.
29.	*Snöfrid* (Rydberg), improvisation for recitation, chorus, and orchestra ...	1900	Helsingfors	H.
30.	*Islossningen i Uleå älv* (Topelius), improvisation for recitation, male chorus, and orchestra	1899	Helsingfors	Ms.
31.	(a) *Song of the Athenians* (Rydberg), for boys' and men's voices, horn septet, and percussion	1899	Helsingfors	B. & H.

Opus	Title	Date	Place	Publisher
31. (b) *Hast thou courage* (Wecksell), for male chorus and orchestra ...		1913	Järvenpää	B. & H.
32. *The Origin of Fire*, for baritone, male chorus, and orchestra		1902	Helsingfors	B. & H.
33. *The Ferryman's Brides* (A. Oksanen), for baritone or mezzo-soprano and orchestra		1897	Lojo	B. & H.
34. Ten little pieces for piano:		1914–16	Järvenpää	B. & H.

Waltz
Dance air
Mazurka
Humoresque
Humoresque
Rêverie
Pastoral Dance
The Harper
Reconnaissance ⎱ added
Souvenir ⎰ later

| **35.** Two songs with piano accompaniment: | | 1907 | Järvenpää | B. & H. |

Jubal (Josephson)
Théodore (Gripenberg)

Opus	Title	Date	Place	Publisher
36.	Six songs with piano accompaniment:	1899	Kervo	B. & H.
	Black Roses (Josephson)			
	But my bird is long in homing (Runeberg)			
	Tennis at Trianon ⎫			
	Ingalill ⎬ (Fröding)			
	March Snow ⎫ (Wecksell)			
	The Diamond ⎭			
37.	Five songs with piano accompaniment:			B. & H.
	The First Kiss (Runeberg) ...	1898	Lojo	
	Berceuse (Topelius) ⎫	1902	Helsingfors	
	Sunrise (Hedberg) ⎭			
	Was it a Dream? (Wecksell)	1902	Tvärminne	
	The Tryst (Runeberg)	1901	Berlin	
38.	Five songs with piano accompaniment:	1904	Tomasby	B. & H.
	Autumn Night ⎫			
	On a Balcony by the Sea ⎪			
	Night ⎬ (Rydberg)			
	The Harper and His Son ⎭			
	I would I were dwelling (Fröding)			

Opus	Title	Date	Place	Publisher
39.	Symphony No. I, in E minor	1898–9	Kervo	B. & H.
40.	Pensées lyriques, for piano:	1912–14	Järvenpää	B. & H.

Valsette
Chanson sans pa-
roles
Humoresque
Menuetto
Berceuse
Pensée mélodique
Rondoletto
Scherzando ⎫
Petite Sérénade ⎬ added later
Polonaise ⎭

Opus	Title	Date	Place	Publisher
41.	Kyllikki, three lyric pieces for piano .	1904	Tomasby	B. & H.
42.	Romance in C major, for string orchestra	1903	Helsingfors	B. & H.
43.	Symphony No. II, in D major	1901	Italy-Lojo	B. & H.
44.	Valse triste, for orchestra, from incidental music to Järnefelt's play Kuolema	1903	Helsingfors	B. & H.
45.	Two pieces for orchestra:	1910	Järvenpää	B. & H.

The Dryads
Dance Intermezzo

Opus	Title	Date	Place	Publisher
46.	Pelléas et Mélisande, suite for small orchestra, from incidental music to Maeterlinck's play:	1905	Järvenpää	S.
	At the Castle Gate			
	A Spring in the Park			
	The Three Blind Sisters			
	Pastorale			
	Mélisande at the Spinning-wheel			
	Entr'acte			
	The Death of Mélisande			
47.	Concerto in D minor, for violin and orchestra, revised in 1905	1903	Lojo	S.
48.	The Captive Queen (P. Cajander), ballad for chorus and orchestra ..	1906	Järvenpää	S.
49.	Pohjola's Daughter, symphonic fantasia for orchestra	1906	Järvenpää	S.
50.	Six songs with piano accompaniment:	1906	Pitkäpaasi (Vederlaks)	S.
	A Song of Spring (Fitger)			

278

Opus	Title	Date	Place	Publisher

50. Six songs with piano accompaniment
— *continued.*

Longing (Weiss)
A Maiden yonder
sings (Susman)
Oh, wert thou here⎫
The Silent Town ⎬ (Dehmel)
The Song of the
Roses (Ritter)

51. *Belshazar's Feast,*
suite for small orchestra, from incidental music to Hjalmar Procopé's play: .... 1906 Järvenpää S.
Oriental Procession
Solitude
Night Music
Khadra's Dance

52. Symphony No. III, in
C major .... 1904–7 Järvenpää S.

53. *Pan and Echo,* dance intermezzo for orchestra, revised in
1909 .... 1906 Järvenpää S.

54. *Swanwhite,* suite for small orchestra, from incidental music to August Strindberg's play: 1908 Järvenpää S.
The Peacock

279

Opus	Title	Date	Place	Publisher
54.	Swanwhite — continued. Listen, the Robin sings Swanwhite Swanwhite and the Prince			
55.	Night-ride and Sunrise, tone-poem for orchestra ...	1909	Järvenpää	S.
56.	Voces intimæ, string quartet	1909	London	S.
57.	Eight songs with piano accompaniment:	1909	Berlin	S.

The Snail
The Wild
  Flower
The Millwheel
May   (Josephson)
The Tree
Baron Magnus
Friendship
The Elf King

58. Ten pieces for piano: 1909   Järvenpää   B. & H.
Rêverie
Scherzino
Air varié
The Shepherd
The Evening
Dialogue
Tempo di menuetto
Fisher Song

Opus	Title	Date	Place	Publisher

58. Ten pieces for piano
— continued.
Sérénade
Summer Song

59. *In Memoriam,* funeral march for orchestra ...... 1909 Järvenpää B. & H.

60. Two songs from Shakspere's *Twelfth Night,* with piano or guitar accompaniment: ..... 1909 Järvenpää B. & H.
Come away, Death
When that I was

61. Eight songs with piano accompaniment: .... 1910 Järvenpää B. & H.
Slow as the colours (Tavaststjerna)
Lapping Waters (Rydberg)
When I dream
Romeo
Romance (Tavaststjerna)
Dolce far niente
Idle Wishes (Runeberg)
The Spell of Springtide (Gripenberg)

Opus	Title	Date	Place	Publisher
62.	(a) Canzonetta for strings	1911	Järvenpää	B. & H.
	(b) Valse romantique for small orchestra			
63.	Symphony No. IV, in A minor	1911	Järvenpää	B. & H.
64.	The Bard, tone-poem for orchestra ...	1913	Järvenpää	B. & H.
65.	Two part-songs for mixed chorus a cappella:			B. & H.
	People of Land and of Sea	1912	Järvenpää	
	Bell Melody of Berghäll Church	1912	Kuhmois	
66.	Scènes historiques, II, suite for orchestra:	1912	Järvenpää	B. & H.
	The Chase			
	Love Song			
	At the Drawbridge			
67.	Three sonatinas for piano	1912	Järvenpää	B. & H.
68.	Two rondinos for piano	1912	Järvenpää	U.
69.	Two serenades for violin and orchestra:			B. & H.
	I, in D minor	1912	Kuhmois	
	II, in G minor	1913	Järvenpää	

Opus	Title	Date	Place	Publisher
70.	Luonnotar (Kalevala), tone-poem for soprano and orchestra	1913	Järvenpää	B. & H.
71.	Incidental music to the pantomime Scaramouche (Poul Knudsen), for small orchestra	1913	Järvenpää	H.

72. Six songs with piano accompaniment: **B. & H.**

	Title	Date	Place
	Farewell (Rydberg)	1914	Berlin
	Orion's Girdle (Topelius)	1914	Järvenpää
	The Kiss (Rydberg)		
	The Echo Nymph (Larin Kyösti) .		
	The Wanderer and the Brook (Greif)	1915	Järvenpää
	A Hundred Ways (Runeberg)		

Opus	Title	Date	Place	Publisher
73.	Aallottaret (The Oceanides), tone-poem for orchestra	1914	Berlin-Järvenpää	B. & H.

283

Opus	Title	Date	Place	Publisher
74.	Four lyric pieces for piano:			B. & H.
	Eclogue	1914	Berlin	
	Soft West Wind ..			
	At the Dance	1914	Järvenpää	
	In the Old Home .			
75.	Five pieces for piano:	1914	Järvenpää	B. & H.
	The Solitary Tree			
	When the Mountain Ash is in flower			
	The Aspen			
	The Birch Tree			
	The Fir Tree			
76.	Thirteen pieces for piano:	1914	Järvenpää	
	Esquisse			
	Étude			
	Carillon			
	Humoresque			
	Consolation			
	Romanzetta			
	Affettuoso			
	Pièce enfantine			
	Arabesque			
	Elegiaco			
	The Twin Flowers of the North			
	Capricietto			
	Harlequinade			

Opus	Title	Date	Place	Publisher
77.	Earnest Melodies for violin or 'cello and orchestra: ..			H.
	Laetare anima mea	1914	Järvenpää	
	Ab imo pectore ...	1915	Järvenpää	
78.	Four pieces for violin (or 'cello) and piano:	1915	Järvenpää	H.
	Impromptu			
	Romance			
	Religioso			
	Rigaudon			
79.	Six pieces for violin and piano:	1915	Järvenpää	H.
	Souvenir			
	Tempo di menuetto			
	Danse caractéristique			
	Sérénade			
	Dance idyll			
	Berceuse			
80.	Sonatina for violin and piano	1915	Järvenpää	H.
81.	Five pieces for violin and piano	1915	Järvenpää	W.
	Mazurka			
	Rondino			
	Valse			
	Aubade			
	Menuetto			

Opus	Title	Date	Place	Publisher
82.	Symphony No. V, in E flat major	1914–15	Järvenpää	H.
83.	Incidental music to Hofmannsthal's *Jedermann*, for small orchestra .	1916	Järvenpää	Ms.
84.	Five part-songs for male voices a cappella: .... Herr Lager, På berget, Ett drömackord, Evige Eros (Fröding) Till havs (Reuter)	1915	Järvenpää	Ms.
85.	Five pieces for piano: Bluebells, The Carnation, The Iris, The Snapdragon, The Campanula	1916	Järvenpää	H.
86.	Six songs with piano accompaniment: Vårförnimmelser (Tavaststjerna), Längtan heter min arvedel (Karlfeldt), Dold förening (Snoilsky), Och finns det en tanke (Tavaststjerna)	1916	Järvenpää	H.

Opus	Title	Date	Place	Publisher
86.	Six songs with piano accompaniment — continued. Sångarlön (Snoilsky) I systrar, I bröder (Lybeck)			
87.	(a) Impromptu for orchestra ...... (b) Humoresk, for violin and orchestra	1917	Järvenpää	H.
88.	Six songs with piano accompaniment: The Anemone The Two Roses (Franzén) The Star-flower The Primrose The Thornbush (Runeberg) The Flower	1917	Järvenpää	H.
89.	Four Humoresques, for violin and orchestra	1917	Järvenpää	H.
90.	Six songs of Runeberg: .... The North Your Message The Morning The Bird-catcher Summer Night What has brought you here?	1917	Järvenpää	B. & H.

287

Opus	Title	Date	Place	Publisher
91.	March of the Finnish infantry	1918	Järvenpää	B. & H.
	Scout March, for orchestra	1918	Järvenpää	
92.	Oma maa (Kallio), cantata for chorus and orchestra ..	1918	Järvenpää	Ms.
93.	Jordens sång, cantata for the inauguration of Åbo University, to words by Jarl Hemmer, for chorus and orchestra	1919	Järvenpää	W.
94.	Six pieces for piano: Dance Novellette Sonnet Berger et Bergerette Mélodie Gavotte	1919	Järvenpää	H.
95.	Maan virsi (Eino Leino), cantata for chorus and orchestra	1920	Järvenpää	H.
96.	Three pieces for orchestra: .... Valse lyrique Autrefois, scène pastorale Valse chevalresque	1920		H.

Opus	Title	Date	Place	Publisher
97. Six Bagatelles for piano:		1920	Järvenpää	B. & H.

Humoresque
Song
Little Waltz
Humorous March
Impromptu
Humoresque

98. (a) Suite mignonne for two flutes and strings		1921	Järvenpää	C.

Petite Scène
Polka
Epilogue

(b) Suite champêtre for strings:		1921	Järvenpää	H.

Pièce caractéristique
Mélodie élégiaque
Danse

99. Eight short pieces for piano:		1922	Järvenpää	F-r.

Pièce humoristique
Esquisse
Souvenir
Impromptu
Couplet
Animoso
Moment de Valse
Petite Marche

Opus	Title	Date	Place	Publisher
100. Suite caractéristique for orchestra ...		1922	Järvenpää	H.
Vivo				
Lento				
Commodo				
101. Five Romantic Compositions, for piano:		1923	Järvenpää	F.
Romance				
Chant du soir				
Scène lyrique				
Humoresque				
Scène romantique				
102. Novellette, for violin and piano		1923	Järvenpää	H.
103. Five Characteristic Impressions, for piano:		1924	Järvenpää	B. & H.
The Village Church				
The Fiddler				
The Oarsman				
The Storm				
In Mournful Mood				
104. Symphony No. VI, in D minor		1923	Järvenpää	A. H.
105. Symphony No. VII, in C major		1924	Järvenpää	H.
106. Five Danses Champêtres, for violin and piano		1925	Järvenpää	F.

Opus	Title	Date	Place	Publisher
107.	Ritual Chorus, with organ accompaniment	1925	Järvenpää	Ms.
108.	Two part-songs for male voices a cappella:	1925	Järvenpää	Ms.

Humoreski \
Ne pitkän } (Larin Kyösti)

109.	Incidental music to Shakspere's *The Tempest*, for orchestra	1926	Järvenpää	H.
110.	*The Song of Väinö* (*Kalevala*), for chorus and orchestra	1926	Järvenpää	Ms.
111.	Two pieces for organ: Intrada Mournful Music	1926	Järvenpää	Ms.
112.	*Tapiola*, symphonic poem for orchestra	1925	Järvenpää	B. & H.
113.	*Musique religieuse*, for solo voice, chorus and organ	1927	Järvenpää	Ms.
114.	Five Esquisses for piano: .... Landscape Winter Scene Forest Lake Song in the Forest Spring Vision	1929	Järvenpää	Ms.

Opus	Title	Date	Place	Publisher
115.	Four compositions for violin and piano: Moods of the Moor Tale Humorous The Bells (Capricietto)	1929	Järvenpää	B. & H.
116.	Three compositions for violin and piano: .... Scène de danse Danse caractéristique Rondeau romantique	1929	Järvenpää	B. & H.

B. *Without opus numbers*

Title	Date	Place	Publisher
Sonata for violin and piano in F major	1886	Helsingfors	Ms.
Piano trio	1887	Korpo	Ms.
The Song of the Watersprite	1888	Helsingfors	Ms.
Nights of Jealousy (Runeberg), recitation with accompaniment	1888	Helsingfors	Ms.
Serenade for voice and piano, to words by Runeberg ..	1888	Helsingfors	Ms.
Theme and variations for string quartet	1888	Helsingfors	Ms.
String suite in A major	1889	Helsingfors	Ms.
String quartet in A minor ..	1889	Helsingfors	Ms.
Piano quintet in G minor ..	1889	Berlin	Ms.
Overture in A minor	1890–1	Vienna	Ms.
Overture in E major	1890–1	Vienna	Ms.
Piano quartet in C major ...	1891	Vienna	Ms.
A Ballet Scene for orchestra	1891	Vienna	Ms.
Tiera, tone-piece for brass band	1894	Helsingfors	Ms.
The Dryad, tone-poem for orchestra	1894	Helsingfors	Ms.
University cantata for 1894 .	1894	Helsingfors	Ms.
Min rastas (Kanteletar), for male chorus	1894	Helsingfors	Otava.

Title	Date	Place	Publisher
Coronation cantata	1895	Helsingfors	Ms.
Rondo for viola and piano ..	1895	Helsingfors	Ms.
The Maiden in the Tower (Cajander) opera in one act	1896	Helsingfors	Ms.
Yks' voima (Cajander), for male chorus	1898	Helsingfors	Otava.
Cortège, for orchestra	1901	Helsingfors	Ms.
Portraits, for string orchestra	1901	Helsingfors	Ms.
The Cavalier, for piano	1901	—	B. & H.
Six Finnish folk-songs for piano	1903	—	B. & H.
Ej med klagan (Runeberg), for mixed chorus	1905	Järvenpää	W.
Carminalia, for boys' voices	1905	Järvenpää	B. & H.
Incidental music to the play The Language of the Birds (Adolf Paul)	1911	—	B. & H.
Drömmarne, for mixed chorus	1912	Järvenpää	
Uusimaa, for mixed chorus .	1912	Järvenpää	
Juhlamarssi, for mixed chorus	1912	Järvenpää	
Päiv ei pääse (Erkko), for children's voices a cappella	1913	Järvenpää	
National school march, for children's voices a cappella	1913	Järvenpää	

Title	Date	Place	Publisher
Koulutie (Koskenniemi), for children's voices a cappella	1913	Järvenpää	
Three songs for American schools, for children's voices a cappella	1913	Järvenpää	
Tanken (Runeberg), for two sopranos, with piano accompaniment	1915	Järvenpää	Ms.
Narcissus (Gripenberg), for voice, with piano accompaniment	1918	Järvenpää	B. & H.
The Sails (Öhqvist), for voice, with piano accompaniment	1918	Järvenpää	B. & H.
Little Girls (Procopé), for voice with piano accompaniment	1918	Järvenpää	B. & H.
Erloschen (Busse-Palmo), for voice, with piano accompaniment	1918	Järvenpää	B. & H.
Veljeni (Aho), for male chorus	1920	Järvenpää	H-m.
Jone havsfärd (Fröding), for male chorus	1920	Järvenpää	H-m.
Likhet (Runeberg), for male chorus	1920	Järvenpää	H-m.
Two songs (Schybergson), for male chorus	1920	Järvenpää	H-m.

JEAN SIBELIUS

Title	Date	Place	Publisher
Pièce romantique for piano .	1920	Järvenpää	B. & H.
Longing	1920	Järvenpää	B. & H.
Andante festivo, for strings	1924	Järvenpää	
Andante lirico, for strings ..	1924	Järvenpää	
Two psalms for mixed chorus	1925–27	Järvenpää	H-m.
N. Y. Laulajat, for male chorus	1929	Järvenpää	
Viborgs Sångarbröder, for male chorus	1929	Järvenpää	
Fridolins dårskap (Karlfeldt), for male chorus			
Sinisorsa (A. V. Koskimies), for voice and piano			
Mandolinata for piano			
Karjalan osa (R. Nurminen)			F-r.

BIBLIOGRAPHY

The following are among the works referred to and consulted:

BUSONI, FERRUCCIO: *Von der Einheit der Musik.* Berlin, 1922.

CASTRÉN, G.: *Juhani Aho.* 2 vols. Helsingfors, 1922.

EDELFELT, B.: *Alexandra Edelfelt.* Helsingfors, 1920.

FLODIN, KARL: *Finska Musiker.* Helsingfors, 1900.

———: *Martin Wegelius.* Helsingfors, 1922.

———: *Musikliv och Reseminnen.* Helsingfors, 1931.

FROSTERUS, S.: "*Sibelius Koordinater.*" (*Nya Argus.*) Helsingfors, 1932.

FURUHJELM, E.: *Jean Sibelius.* Borga, 1916.

Gallén-Kallelan Muisto. Borga, 1932.

GRAY, CECIL: *Sibelius.* London, 1931.

JÄRNEFELT, A.: *Vanhempieni Romaani.* Vol. II. Helsingfors, 1922.

KONOW, WALTER VON: "*Muistoja Jean Sibeliuksen Poikavuosilta.*" (*Aulos, säveltaiteelliskirjallinen julkaisu.*) Helsingfors, 1925.

KOTILAINEN, OTTO: "*Mestarin Muokattavana.*" (*Aulos.*) Helsingfors, 1925.

Litchfield County Choral Union, 1900–1912. 2 vols. Norfolk, 1912.

MADETOJA, LEEVI: " Jean Sibelius Opettajana." (Aulos.) Helsingfors, 1925.

NEWMARCH, ROSA: Mary Wakefield. A Memoir. London, 1911.

NIEMANN, WALTER: Jean Sibelius. Leipzig, 1917.

PAUL, ADOLF: En Bok om en Människa. Stockholm, 1890.

SELDEN-GOTH, G.: Ferruccio Busoni. Leipzig, 1922.

SÖDERHJELM, WERNER: Profiler. Helsingfors, 1923.

The majority of Sibelius's letters quoted in this book were addressed to Baron Axel Carpelan, a highly educated man and a distinguished personality, who was one of Sibelius's most intimate friends and his constant confidant in musical matters from the summer of 1900 until his death in the spring of 1919. Sibelius has commemorated their friendship in the dedication of his second symphony.

INDEX

i

INDEX

viii

INDEX